BEWARE...

You are about to enter an ESCAPE BOOK. If you don't know what one of those is, then perhaps I should explain. An Escape Book is a form of puzzle book in which the unwary reader may become trapped for eternity. It is an escape room in the form of a book. You can decide on your own path, but your choice is often controlled by the solutions you give to the puzzles you encounter along the way. You must solve the puzzles to escape the pages.

Some puzzles will offer you alternative routes according to your solution. Others will invite you to calculate the next entry you should turn to. When this happens, you should check the "from" number to ensure that you came from the right location and are still on the right path. If you have arrived from the wrong place, you should turn back and think again.

Not all wrong solutions will end the story. As befits an adventure in which you play the role of Sherlock Holmes, this book is far more cunning than that. Some wrong answers may have unforeseen consequences further down the path, causing you to miss a helpful clue or even land a red herring.

While you are trapped inside the Escape Book, you should pay attention to everything you see. Once the game is afoot, there are all manner of clues hidden on the pages. Use Watson's Notebook – which you will discover shortly – to record your observations. Some of these notes might be needed to solve later puzzles. You will also be required to master the Code Wheel, located on the cover of the book (of which, more later). If you are struggling with your art of deduction, you will find some helpful hints and clues (and even the answers) located at 221A and 221B at the back of the book.

There is more than one door through which you can exit the Escape Book. Some doors are marked with success... others with infamy. Only the most observant of detectives will find an escape route that results in newspaper headlines proclaiming their heroic success.

▶ *These arrows direct you to your next entry.*
Now, all great adventures begin by turning the first page...

WATSON'S NOTEBOOK

Use this notebook to jot down anything of interest you encounter during your adventure; you may find it helps you to solve a later puzzle.

Pay particular attention to the TIME. You are in a race against the clock, but you may also find that the clock is your friend:

	:	
	:	
	:	
	:	
	:	

Sometimes you might have only the hour or the minutes, but they are still worth recording in the table above. (NOTE: unlike Italy, Britain has not yet embraced Sir Sandford Fleming's proposal to use the 24-hour clock, so you and Watson should continue to use only the 12-hour clock).

Hidden in the Escape Book are two passages from Sherlock Holmes' original adventures. Should you discover them, note them here.

1 ....

2 ....

NOTES & OBSERVATIONS

....

....

....

....

....

....

....

....

Holmes believes the key to this adventure can be found in three parts. On their own, they might not make sense, but once we've found them all we might avoid unlocking doors we do not wish to pass through.

Holmes asked that I bring along my Periodic Table.
(It can be found at the back of this book.)

▶ *If you have yet to begin your adventure – Turn over the page*
(Feel free to refer to Watson's Notebook at any time.)

THE STORY

In the upcoming adventure, you will take on the role of the world's most famous consulting detective, Sherlock Holmes, as he becomes trapped within a dastardly plot. You will see everything from his point of view, you will attempt to solve the puzzles with his powers of deduction, you will *be* him! You might even find a magnifying glass helpful. So, try to think in the way that Sherlock thinks. As he/you once said, in Sir Arthur Conan Doyle's *The Sign of the Four* (1890): "When you have eliminated the impossible, whatever remains, HOWEVER IMPROBABLE, must be the truth."

You will be accompanied, of course, by your faithful companion Doctor John H. Watson. He will offer you words of advice, a voice of reason and a steady hand on a revolver in times of peril. You should also make good use of his notebook to record observations that may help with your escape.

The adventure is set in a real pumping station, the London Waterworks of the title, which today has become the London Museum of Water and Steam (www.waterandsteam.org.uk) at Kew Bridge. The chimney has been taken down (it had developed an alarming lean, and earned the local nickname of the Leaning Tower of Brentford) and water is no longer pumped into London from the site, but the beam engines are still there and furthermore you can visit them and see them in glorious steam. The standpipe tower remains, as it was in Holmes' time, an elegant landmark by the river.

If you search the 1880s archives of the Old Bailey – where Newgate Gaol was located at the time of this adventure – you can read some of the words of the real Mr Sidney Robert Smith in the court transcripts. Oddly, he never mentions his involvement with the dreadful events in the pumping station or his encounter with those two most special gentlemen, Sherlock Holmes and Doctor Watson...

THE CODE WHEEL

Set into the cover of the Escape Book is a Code Wheel, which is an essential part of your equipment for solving some of the puzzles you will encounter. It features a series of windows behind which are letters, numbers and a sequence of figures containing a semaphore code from *The Adventure of the Dancing Men* (1903), and can be used in a number of ways:

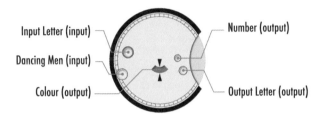

Input Letter (input)

Dancing Men (input)

Colour (output)

Number (output)

Output Letter (output)

You can find a digital version of the Code Wheel at:
www.ammonitepress.com/gift/sherlock-code-wheel

In some puzzles you'll discover coded messages in the form of unintelligible notes, strings of random numbers or secret symbols hidden in the story. Using the Code Wheel, input your discoveries in the relevant *input* dial, then decode them by reading the relevant *output* dial. Sometimes there are multiple steps in decoding a puzzle – perhaps the Dancing Men reveal a word, which then displays a colour. To begin your adventure, you must first unlock the Escape Book. To do this, you should use the Code Wheel to solve the following cipher:

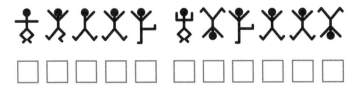

▶ *The secret code should reveal the location where your adventure begins. Once you have solved the puzzle and discovered the location – Turn to 1*

221B BAKER STREET

The rain has stopped and the clouds are already parting to reveal a yellow, fingernail moon. You look from the bow window to the far side of the street, where a curious-looking couple are standing in the dim light of the gas lamp. Doctor Watson joins you, his curiosity piqued.

"Do you know them, Holmes?" he asks.

"I do not," you reply, "but the young woman is clearly here to deliver some sort of document."

A moment later, the woman is hurrying across to the door below with an envelope in her hand. Her companion watches her, and then slowly lifts his head to look up at you. He is wearing a long coat and his broad arms are holding a heavy bundle wrapped in what appears to be a blanket. The man's face is hidden by the shadow of his wide-brimmed hat.

"I don't like the look of that cove," mutters Watson.

You hear the flap of the letter-box downstairs. Across the road, the man has already turned and is marching away into the London gloom. The woman hurries to catch up with him.

"Mrs Hudson has already retired for the night. Watson, would you mind?"

"Not at all," says your companion, hurrying off to collect the envelope.

The envelope contains a note. It has been torn, in a manner suggesting precision. In stark contrast, the envelope in which it was delivered is intact and uncreased.

▶ *Study the note carefully before turning to 104*

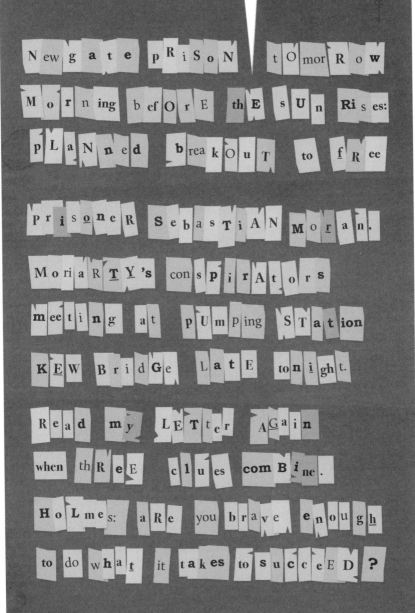

Newgate pRiSoN tOmorRow
Morning befOrE thE sUn Ri es:
pLANNed breakOUT to fRee

PrisoneR SebaSTiAN Moran.

MoriaRTY's conspirAtors
meeting at pUmping StAtion
KEW BridGe LatE tonight.

Read my LETter AGain
when thReE clues comBine.

HoLmes: aRe you brave enough
to do what it takes tosucceED?

THE ADVENTURE OF THE LONDON WATERWORKS

I peered through the glass at a minuscule mark that looked like a dark-blue smear. Gradually, it resolved itself into two words: "HELP ME".

Holmes bellowed a summons to Mrs Hudson. "Pray, Mrs Hudson, what's the name of our laundry?"

"Rastroy's Superior Laundry and Bagwash Company," quavered Mrs Hudson. "It's a new establishment, set up by Mrs Jemima Rastroy – the poor widow of Major Rastroy who perished so heroically at Maiwand." Mrs Hudson's lip trembled. "She said that he knew and admired you, Doctor Watson."

"Yes, yes," said Holmes testily, "Where is the confounded place?"

"Little Drummond Street, sir, very near Euston Station."

"Is it now? Come, Watson!" he cried jovially, snatching up his loaded riding crop. "The game's afoot. You can bet your shirt on it."

As the hansom rattled east along the Marylebone Road, I pondered aloud: "I've been cudgelling my brains, but have no recollection of Major Rastroy. War does funny things to a chap's memory but even so... it's a real puzzle."

Holmes looked up from his incessant doodling. His eyes narrowed. "What name did Mrs Hudson give for this enigmatic washerwoman, Watson?"

"Jenny. No, Jemima. Mrs Jemima Rastroy."

Holmes scribbled down the name. Suddenly he burst out laughing. "Capital!" he chortled. "Watson, once again in your own plain-speaking way you have led us directly to the solution."

I confess, I did not know what on Earth he was gibbering about.

▶ *Turn to 81*

MORIARTY'S HOODLUMS

The noise of your pursuers' heavy footfalls echoes down the tunnel. The uneven ground – treacherous with rails, debris, lumps of coal and pooled water – impedes the hunters as well the hunted. But the scurrying rats disrupt your concentration.

"How many killers does Moriarty have at his disposal?" pants Watson.

"It's an interesting question, Watson," you reply, your hawk-like eyes darting about in search of rats. "My Irregulars have over the years gathered some very specific information about his operation, and I can tell you this. Moriarty teaches the hoodlums in his inner circle four distinct methods of killing: poisoning, marksmanship, strangulation and knife-work. Every hoodlum in his inner circle knows exactly two of those methods."

"That seems... oddly specific," gasps the doctor.

"Moriarty is a professor of mathematics, Watson, so he cannot help himself. But it is that exact weakness that lets us calculate the number of hoodlums in his inner circle. Because – and this, my dear friend, is the key – it also ensures that, whichever pair of methods you pick, there will be one, and only one, hoodlum who is trained in both of them."

Watson stops and catches his breath, and then shakes his head.

"Holmes could you just tell me roughly how many of these hoodlums he has?"

▶ *"Fewer than 7" – Turn to 65*

▶ *"More than 7" – Turn to 77*

(4) AN INSOLENT GIANT

Your step down onto the stone flags, their slight unevenness exaggerated by the powder-shadows of coal dust. You pass racks of tools, tubs of grease and a pair of tar barrels. There is a cabinet that contains a neat row of labelled bottles, which immediately attract your attention because you have more than a passing interest in the chemical sciences. Sadly, you don't have the time to inspect them.

You slink between the boilers and the noise of the furnaces keeps your footsteps hidden. You're close enough now to inspect the giant man who is still shovelling coal into the firebox of one of the boilers.

All of a sudden, the giant boilerman stops his work, straightens up – revealing himself to be a whole head taller than you – and stares in your direction. You're caught in the open and have no time to hide. Rather than getting flustered, you nod in an attempt to be civil while prudently maintaining your distance. The boilerman hefts his shovel into both his huge hands in a way that suggests it's not just coal that he plans to throw around. He offers a faint smile. Clearly he's been expecting you.

Watson coughs awkwardly, and the two of you decide to continue your traversal of the boiler house to the external door. The stoker makes no attempt to stop you, insolently watching you both as you walk through his domain.

When you reach the door, instead of finding your freedom, you discover a clock-like contraption attached to it, with wires through both the door handle and hinges, attached to a collection of flasks and tubes clearly marked EXPLOSIVE. Exit is not going to be straightforward.

▶ *Examine the contraption – Turn to 110*

A FALSE START

Watson looks a little bemused as you walk away from the obvious entrance, but he follows anyway. The outer wall seems to stretch on forever and there appears to be no other way in. All of a sudden you spot another gate. Your instincts were correct.

Unfortunately, your joy is short-lived as it's clear you've looped back around to the main entrance. It's very unlike you to make such a mistake.

Suddenly you are aware of a presence behind you, but it's too late for you to react. It's your second mistake in as many minutes.

▶ *Everything goes black – Turn to 111*

THE WRONG WIRE

You inspect the contraption. It is not as complicated as it first looked and you deduce that if you work clockwise, removing the wires in turn, it should bypass the clock. The only question is which wire is your start point?

Beginning at the top, you slowly detach the first wire. Sadly, you've miscalculated the complexity of the mechanism and the wires and cogs of the contraption tug away at the stoppers and tip up the flasks.

"Get away from it!" cries Watson as he jumps clear. You follow suit, leaping back and away from the infernal device just as it explodes. You are thrown to the floor by the blast, showered with debris and shrouded in a billowing cloud of smoke. The explosion has now blocked your exit through the door.

On a normal day you wouldn't have let such a trap get the better of you. Staggering to your feet, you and Watson return to the office.

▶ *In the office – Turn to 67*

⑦ A HALF-FINISHED WORD PUZZLE

There is a single, brown folder in the "H" drawer. You lift it out and go to place it on the desk. But there's a newspaper in the way; as you are about to move it aside, you notice a partially completed word puzzle. Evidently, the steam engine is so reliable that the nights here are spent passing the time with such distractions.

As Watson goes about trying to revive the poor man – who is still out cold – you pull back the chair and sit down at the desk.

Watson looks up, exasperated "How are you so dashed calm, Holmes? Someone has just trapped us in here and nearly killed this fellow. And you are proposing to sit and do word puzzles? It may have escaped your notice, but someone might be trying to kill us!"

"Someone is trying to trap us, not kill us," you explain calmly. "We might know more when you can ask our unconscious friend a few questions, and meanwhile I will go about the business of using my intellect."

The puzzle is partially obscured by a sooty thumbprint, but it should still be possible to complete it. Set the Code Wheel to the SEVENTH LETTER of the solution to 9 Across. If you are flustered by the situation, you could guess... but Sherlock Holmes does not guess.

9 Across:

⬛⬛⬛⬛⬛⬛⬛⬛⬛⬛⬛

▲

▶ *If the Code Wheel shows blue – Turn to 97*

▶ *If the Code Wheel shows green – Turn to 59*

▶ *If the Code Wheel shows yellow – Turn to 99*

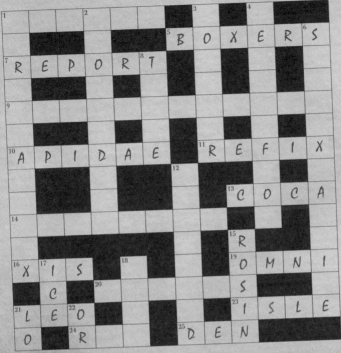

Across

1 See 24 Across
5 Pugilists (4)
... (12)
13 Cocaine shrub (4)
14/3 A pale warrior beheld ironclads in chaos (8,7)
16 14th letters of the Greek alphabet (3)
19 Prefix for all (4)
20 See 8 Down
21 August zodiac (3)
23 Land surrounded by water (4)
24/1 Crimson ring (3,6)
25 Lair (3)

Down

1 Container made of stiff paper (9,3)
2 Bent male person (7,3)
3 See 14 Across
4 On the end of Satan's leg (6,4)
6 Blood-sucker from southern English county (6,7)
8/20 Triangular brick walls under the end of roofs, tripled (5,6)
12/18 Spotted strip (8,4)
15 Pine naptha for violin (5)
17 Frozen water (3)
18 See 12 Down
21 See! (2)
22 Otherwise, gold (2)

from 14

⑧ GETTING LATE

You congratulate yourself for the way you're solving all these puzzles, but wonder about the time. You flip open your pocket watch. Either your watch is wrong or it's getting late: twenty past one in the morning!

▶ *Smoke your cherrywood pipe – Turn to 38*

⑨ THE CROWS' CLUE

from 18

Watson pauses, and you turn to face him.

"I don't know what predicament we might be about to get into, Sherlock," he says. "But whatever it is, it's reassuring to know you are on top of your game. Good show, sir!"

"From the way these crows have been disturbed, Watson," you reply. "I deduce that there are a number of unwelcome strangers over yonder. We should enter quickly through these gates and no others."

▶ *You head towards the gates – Turn to 84*

⑩ A MAN BOUND IN IRON

from 12

The trapdoor in the chequer-plate flooring reveals a metal ladder running down to the suction well of the Boulton & Watt engine room. That's where the water is offered up to the mighty engine, the water that is being pumped out and away into London. It's as cold as the river that feeds it, but darker, amongst the foundations of the engine house. But as you peer in, and your eyes accustom to the gloom, an upturned face swims into view, looking back at you: a face framed by spectacular, greying mutton-chop sideburns. Its owner calls out to you but his voice is hard to make out over the echoes of the sloshing water.

Watson slides down the ladder first, and you follow, stepping onto the concrete walkway around the open pool. As you hurry around to the opposite side, the true horror of the scene is revealed. The mutton-chopped man is bound from chest to toe in heavy, industrial chains, swathing him completely in iron. His outstretched arms are chained to the thick pipes that run along the walls, so that he appears the victim of some infernal medieval torture.

"Good heavens, man," cries Watson to the poor fellow, "how did you come to be like this? And who are you, sir?"

You concentrate in order to hear his reply over the rhythmic noise of the pump and the water. For a man chained to a wall in the suction well of a pumping station, he is remarkably composed.

"Sidney Robert Smith," he shouts politely over the watery racket. "Governor of Newgate Gaol. I'd offer you a hand, gentlemen, but, as you can see, I am compromised." And he tries to raise an arm, even a little, but he is so thoroughly run-around with heavy chains that he cannot move at all.

"I am Sherlock Holmes, consulting detective."

He almost smiles. "Indeed. I was told you would be along. Pleased to meet you, sir."

"Hmm. And this is Doctor John Watson, who will release you. Watson?"

▶ *Talk to the governor – Turn to 76*

(11) FOCUS

from 18

Watson pauses, and you turn to face him.

"I don't know what we might be about to get into, Sherlock," he says. "But whatever it is, I need you to be on the top of your game. Focus!"

You have no idea what he means. Unless, perhaps, you made a mistake counting those crows?

▶ *You head towards the gates – Turn to 84*

(12) A TRAPDOOR

from 90

You walk to the river-end of the machine, where the engine draws up water from beneath the chequer-plate floor. There's a trapdoor beneath your feet. It's not a secret trapdoor – if there are any of those in the pumping station, you've yet to discover them – but offers access for the engine crew to get below the engine.

▶ *Lift the trapdoor – Turn to 10*

(13) AN INFERNAL DEVICE

from 53

You had expected to fling open the door and jump through, but it won't open easily. A weight has been added to the outside, and the hinges have been stiffened. As you push against it, you see the wires and cogs of the contraption tug away at the stoppers and tip up the flasks.

"Get away from it!" cries Watson as he jumps clear. You follow suit, leaping back and away from the infernal device just as it explodes...

You are thrown to the floor by the blast, showered with debris and shrouded in a billowing cloud of smoke. Almost immediately, you hear the door slamming shut again and the tinkle of glass and metal fragments bouncing off the metal boilers. You have had a lucky escape. When everything is quiet, the sound of the giant stoker's laughter echoes around the room.

Staggering to your feet, you and Watson return to the office.

▶ *In the office – Turn to 67*

from 38

(14) THE BLACK NOTEBOOK

The cover of the notebook is completely blank: there's no writing, pattern or label. When you flick through it, all the pages but one seem empty – that one exception, indicated by a folded corner, has writing on it:

> *Find me on the cover*
> *Ransomed Cork*
> *Hostaged Plug*
> *Blackmailed Bung*

It's a curious puzzle. You look at the cover of the book in your hands. You intuitively know that the author's clue is staring you in the face, but sitting in the office you just cannot see it. You drum your fingers on the desk and berate yourself. Why are you being so doltish?

▶ *Ransomed Cork – Turn to 23*

▶ *Hostaged Plug – Turn to 68*

▶ *Blackmailed Bung – Turn to 8*

Remember Gloria Scott
Grand Junction Water Works.

ENGINEER SITE REPORT DOCKET

Site: Kew GJWW
Date of inspection: 10 September
Superintendent: J Caruthers

Our engineers have reported to you
that they found evidence that the
topmost spinning governor is not yet
regulating pressures below $20\,\text{lbf}^2$,
causing the accumulation of steam in
the engine inlet pipes.

15 THE ENGINEER'S DOCKET

You've solved the code of the punched letters, but that's not the only puzzle amongst the documents you took from the safe.

Another jumps out at you: it's an engineer's docket, and it has a name you recognize scrawled in a message at the top, written in what appears to be lipstick. You read the words aloud:

"Remember Gloria Scott."

Watson looks up. "That name sounds familiar," he says.

"Indeed it should," you reply. "The *Gloria Scott* was a ship, and the key to one of my first cases. I told you about it once. Back while I was at university, and long before we met, I was called to the home of a friend, Victor Trevor. His father had died after suffering a stroke, the cause of which was apparently a letter he had received in the post. The letter was seemingly trivial, certainly not grotesque enough to cause such a reaction. Had I missed something? If there were a hidden meaning in it, I was confident that I could pluck it forth. For an hour I sat pondering over it in the gloom, until at last a weeping maid brought in a lamp, and close at her heels came my friend Trevor, pale but composed. I dare say my face looked as bewildered as yours did just now when first I read the message. Then I reread it very carefully. It was evidently as I had thought, and some secret meaning must lie buried in this strange combination of words. I tried it backwards, but the combination was not encouraging. Then I tried alternate words, but they failed to throw any light upon it. And then in an instant the key of the riddle was in my hands, and I saw that every third word, beginning with the first, would give a message which might well drive old Trevor to despair."

You look at the engineer's docket, and search for the hidden message.

▶ *When you have extracted the concealed message – Turn to 91*

(16) THE SUMATRAN RAT PUZZLE

from 61

The light flares up and a hundred eyes reflect the spark back at you. Rats. A lot of rats. They had been creeping out of the crevices and coming up through the drains, attracted by the unusual presence of people.

Of course there are rats down here. Lean rats, plump rats, aggressive rats, timid rats, cunning rats, diseased rats, sewer rats: all kinds of London rat. You realize it must be inevitable to find seething colonies of them down here nearer to the river – and that, of course, is where this tunnel leads.

Watson is unperturbed by rats – his military experience has inured him to far worse afflictions than a mere rodent presence – but you are reminded of the especially unpleasant business you had with the GIANT RAT OF SUMATRA. That case was troubling because it was almost paranormal in its resolution. You experience the tiniest shiver down your spine as you remember the adventure and its possible consequences.

You are, famously, a man who is not at the whim of irrational matters such as a superstitious fear of a monstrous rat. And yet, is it just possible that, at this very moment – as you hear the blood racing in your ears – it stems not just from exertion, as you hurry on your way, but from some remote hex cast by the begetter of that Sumatran rodent? Does its influence still haunt you?

Does every rat in the tunnel have an identical match?

▶ *If you think every rat you see has a twin – Turn to 3*

▶ *If you prefer to say that not all the rats are paired – Turn to 80*

THE PRESSURE GAUGE PUZZLE

You quickly scan the gauges on the pipes. Some are broken, and their needles are not showing any value. Others appear still to be operational, and they indicate how much steam is passing through.

The steam is under pressure, and travels in only one direction through the pipes; there are no signs of any leaks that might cause the numbers not to add up.

You quickly deduce that if a gauge shows a number, the next two gauges – that is, one on each of the two pipes it is feeding directly into – should add up to that number. Sometimes, where two pipes feed into one gauge, that gauge should show the total of the two pipes' steam added together. And so on, down through the system.

Watson stares in perplexity at the pipes. To relieve the pressure, in every sense, you must work out how much steam is in the system.

"What is the number on that last dial? Can you work it out, Holmes?"

Of course you can. You're Sherlock Holmes.

You have one minute to solve this.

▶ *If you can work out the final dial in time, turn to that number*

▶ *If you fail to correctly guess the final dial in time – Turn to 85*

(18) THE TOWER

The carriage wheels splash through puddles dotting the damp streets. Residential London is already sleeping, and the houses you see are mostly dark. Candles have been snuffed out and curtains drawn. When you are halfway across Kew Bridge, you call to the driver to halt the cab, hand him the fare and disembark. The Thames is a black strip below you. There are some barges tied up and a few river-people going about their evening's nautical business. As the cab rattles away, Watson leans over the parapet to watch a couple of flat-capped boys bumping a skiff along the bank. On one of the barges, a boatman lowers a lamp that was hanging from a mast and extinguishes it. People do put out their lights before bedding down for the night, so you've probably just witnessed a regular twilight event.

Or a signal, perhaps...

It's usually impossible to tell the two apart. But as you turn towards the pumping station – your destination – you see an orange light flash in reply, near the top of the tower.

Watson sees it too.

"Dashed odd to have windows up a chimney," he says. He often surprises you with how he thinks. You had been considering the signal, not the architecture. Never mind.

"That's not the chimney, Watson. It's the standpipe tower, with stairs all the way up inside it. The chimney is the shorter one, set further back." You pause. "With smoke coming out of it."

You stride towards the pumping station, and Watson, as ever, follows close behind. You wonder at the large number of crows in the sky.

▶ *If you count an even number of crows – Turn to 9*

▶ *If you see an odd number of crows – Turn to 11*

from 22

(19) WATSON'S JUDGEMENT

Bounding up the stairs, you enter the office. Watson is waiting for you and shuts the door as soon as you're through. He looks at you oddly, as if he's disappointed in you. It's a fleeting glance and, besides, you have more important things to do than worry about Watson's judgemental opinion.

▶ *Back in the office – Turn to 49*

(20) MURKY DREAMS

from 34, 41, 73

Tonight, your dreams – so often crystal-clear visions of flight through multi-storeyed palaces of thought – are murky and confused.

When you awake – after much longer than you intended – your face is on the pile of documents on the desk, and there is movement outside.

▶ *Turn to 67*

(21) A MOMENT OF DOUBT

from 38

It is rare for you to suffer from doubt, but – in a moment so brief that Watson doesn't even realize you are indulging in self-reflection – you pause to wonder if you are doing the right thing. If there are any puzzles on the desk that you haven't yet attempted, something tells you that you won't be getting the chance to come back to them.

▶ *Sit back down at the desk – Turn to 38*

▶ *No, you're certain you want to get on – Turn to 90*

▶ *You decide to relax until the morning, for inspiration – Turn to 67*

A MAZE IN A DRAWER

The wooden board that forms the bottom of the drawer has a maze-like pattern scratched into it.

Watson hurries past you and up the stairs. "Don't loiter, Holmes!" he chides as he passes.

You have 15 SECONDS before the giant stoker is upon you!

You don't need a stopwatch: "Holmes and Watson" takes one second to say distinctly. So, count "Holmes and Watson ONE, Holmes and Watson TWO, Holmes and Watson THREE..." as you set about trying to solve the maze.

▶ *If you solved the maze within 15 seconds – Turn to 19*

▶ *If you did not solve the maze in time – Turn to 50*

(23) A SECRET MESSAGE

A scrap of paper, unnoticed on first viewing, falls out of the notebook.
Perhaps it concerns the original note (1) that you have in your pocket:

> 🔑 *Read the letters from the end
> of the note to the start*

On its own, that doesn't seem to make any sense. You stroke your chin
thoughtfully. Is this going to be a three-pipe problem?

▶ *Smoke your pipe – Turn to 38*

(24) A RACE AGAINST TIME

Even as you finish your calculations, the glass in one of the valves shatters.

Moments later, steam begins to jet out of one of the pipes. Perhaps the
increasing pitch of the hissing means other things are about to break.

"I don't think we can linger in here, Holmes," says Watson, in high
agitation. "It's getting dangerous."

He's right, of course. But you've noticed an engineering drawing poking
from the front pocket of the engineer's overalls. You gently extract it.

Perhaps it can be of assistance in deducing what has been happening here.
You study the labyrinthine pattern of pipes.

The hissing increases. Pressure is building in the system. But you can't help but spend time solving the puzzle it presents. Such is the affliction of a mind predisposed to chronic curiosity.

You have FIFTEEN SECONDS to solve the maze!

You don't need a stopwatch: "Holmes and Watson" takes one second to say distinctly. So, count "Holmes and Watson ONE, Holmes and Watson TWO, Holmes and Watson THREE..." as you tackle the maze.

▶ *If you solve the maze in fewer than 15 seconds – Turn to 70*

▶ *If you fail to solve the maze in 15 seconds – Turn to 55*

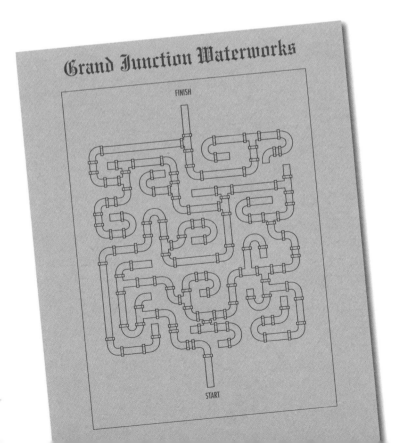

THE UNDERLINED LETTERS

You look at the original note (1) once more. Some of the letters are underlined. They spell out a number.

► *Turn to the number you have discovered*

221B BAKER STREET

"Who's that Holmes?" I asked idly as I fiddled with my shirt collar, which was being confoundedly recalcitrant. Holmes stood at the bay window, smiling in his infuriating manner at the bespattered figure scurrying down Baker Street.

"That, my dear Watson, is Sir Pumfrey James. Does he not resemble in every particular an owl in mourning?" Holmes' eyes danced. He had been in one of his lethargic stupors for the past week, but now he was positively scintillating.

"Sir Pumfrey is something in the Mint. He is much exercised as his Master Printer, a Mr Caslon Gill, has been missing since Friday. We must proceed with stealth to avoid a run on the bank if Gill has been suborned or is under duress to produce undetectable forgeries. What the devil are you doing with that collar, Watson? Stop fiddling, it is deuced annoying. A man cannot deliver a cogent exposition while you are trying to strangulate yourself."

"I can't get the bally thing to do up – and it's just back from the laundry."

Holmes applied himself to the problem. "My dear fellow, of course it won't do up: it's two sizes too small for your rugger neck." He pulled the collar off, and showed me. I was about to rant off to Mrs Hudson about her appalling choice of laundresses, when Holmes whipped out his magnifying glass.

"Great heavens, Watson," he cried, "observe!"

► *Turn to 2*

A CODE IN THE FLOORBOARDS

Well, your powers of observation are still intact. You tuck the note back into your pocket, and suddenly have a thought.

"Watson, have we looked beneath the rug?"

The doctor shakes his head. "It has thus far escaped our attention."

Watson lifts up a corner of the rug. A somewhat sinister sequence of chalked figures is revealed. You are familiar with all manner of secret writings. Indeed, you are the author of a trifling monograph upon the subject, in which you analyse 160 separate ciphers. But this is entirely new to you. If time were not so pressing you would be able to relish the challenge more, but that is of no matter. You apply your methods.

▶ *Turn to the number spelled out by the Dancing Men*

from 56

You put down the postcard. There is going to be more puzzle-solving to do here, you are sure, so you take your pipe from your pocket before spreading upon the desk some more items from the safe.

▶ *Light your pipe – Turn to 38*

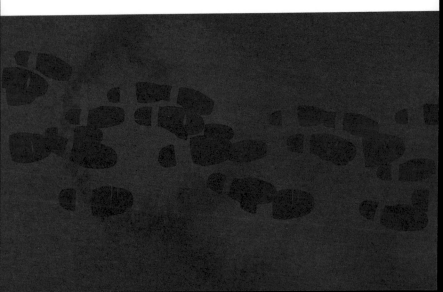

FOOTPRINTS

You jump out of the boiler house. You're free of the building!

Watson follows one second later and heaves on the door to try to shut it, but its stiff hinges won't be rushed.

"What the deuce are you doing, Holmes?" he demands, when he sees you staring at the ground. He's in a hurry to get away from Moriarty's hoodlums – including that giant stoker, presumably – but you are stock-still, examining the footprints out here in the light mud of the yard.

It is hard to tell because there's only a dim lantern illuminating the ground, but you're looking to see if all the recent footprints here are accounted for. Are the prints here just those of the engineer's murderer, the giant stoker and the watchman? Or are there more of Moriarty's henchmen at large?

▶ *These prints could be from only 3 pairs of boots – Turn to 45*

▶ *There are at least 4 different pairs of footprints here – Turn to 103*

from 86

(30) NO CHIME

You set the clock hands to the position and feel a tinge of disappointment when there's no chime or click to suggest anything has changed.

Do you open the door?

▶ *Yes, open the door – Turn to 29*

▶ *No, go back and set the hands again – Turn to 86*

from 89

(31) BOOBY-TRAPPED

You stand up and make a declaration: "Watson, I think we need to try that booby-trapped door."

Watson looks at you uncertainly. "Do you know what time to set the clock-hands to, in order to disarm it?" he asks.

"My dear doctor," you reply, "I have set my mind to it. That, surely, is enough for us both to be confident about escaping alive."

"Good to hear it." He is a loyal fellow, after all.

"Although... I'd appreciate you keeping an eye on that mountain of a stoker while I'm about it."

You leave the office by the door that leads into the boiler house.

▶ *Go back into the boiler house – Turn to 87*

A NARROW ESCAPE

You slam the door behind you as the steam engine threatens to blow. Back in the office, you pause to catch your breath. With no idea how to fix the Maudslay engine, you hope the problem will just sort itself out. The look on Watson's face suggests otherwise.

"I think we should get out, and alert the police," says Watson.

You're still bothered by the message from Moriarty about not having found the governor – whatever that means. But Watson is right: this is a murder scene and you would be better doing your thinking far away from it. Scotland Yard can go about their unimaginative work here instead.

Watson opens the door into the other engine room – the one on the right – and looks in. The Boulton & Watt engine is working away in there. But, just as with the Maudslay engine room, there is no external door.

"Dash it all, Holmes, there are no exits from these engine rooms on either side, so we are obliged to go through the boiler house."

But still your detective mind is distracted. You take the torn note (1) from your pocket and look at it once more.

Some of the letters have a nick beneath them...

▶ *Consult the torn note and turn to the number you discover*

MORIARTY'S INFLUENCE

from 64

In every plot hatched, in every plan executed, you see Professor Moriarty. Behind every endeavour of yours that has not paid off, every attempt at greatness thwarted, you suspect his interference. Every eye that turns towards you when you walk through London, every ear that listens to your conversations, every back that is suspiciously turned when you are out and about in busy public places – every one of those surely belongs to one of his network of informers. This paranoia has gone too far. Now you're even seeing him in word puzzles in which he is not present.

"Holmes, my dear chap, whatever is the matter?"

Watson is turning towards you, a concerned look on his face. But you know that is exactly the artificial concern he would wear were he to be an agent of Moriarty. Of course! The ideal place to install one of his own men, the shared rooms of 221B Baker Street, in the heart of your operations. Was Watson working for Moriarty before he even met you? Or did the professor find a way to turn him once he was in?

You back away as Watson reaches out to you, feigning the concern that a good doctor might have, and then the room spins around and your knees buckle.

When you open you eyes you are back in the office, sitting in the chair. Watson has put a blanket around you, and tells you that you've been unconscious for several hours. He sees you stirring and holds a mug out towards you, steam rising from its contents, wafting its characteristic aroma to your keen nose. You try to remember the circumstances that led you this far, but your memory palace has been ransacked and you cannot fix your mind on anything that went before.

You recognize the smell, though. It's cocoa.

▶ *Drink the hot cocoa – Turn to 67*

COMMONPLACE

The more you look through the diary, the more you are forced to conclude that there is nothing remarkable about it at all. The man's days are repetitive and without much surprise or variation. Perhaps when engineering is well-managed, this is the way things are: regular, unexceptional, predictable.

But this discovery makes you suspicious. As you once told your companion Doctor Watson, "There is nothing so unnatural as the commonplace." So, you redouble your efforts and study the foreman's diary with heightened levels of concentration. But there is nothing redeeming about this document, and before long your eyelids are heavy and your head nodding.

▶ *Fall asleep – Turn to 20*

WATSON'S DISCRETION

The safe door remains resolutely shut. Watson coughs awkwardly, and pretends extreme fascination with the dirt beneath one of his fingernails. His discretion is admirable.

▶ *Try again – Turn to 96*

THE MAIN OFFICE

"No, Watson," you say. "Cocoa! Spilled cocoa. That is all."

Watson continues on into the office. It is a tall but windowless room lit by a lamp. The rug on the floor appears to have been disturbed, as if something heavy has been dragged over it. You observe two more spots of cocoa, and automatically extrapolate the path their position implies.

There is a desk with some books, ledgers and a newspaper on it. Opposite the desk is a row of filing cabinets. In a corner of the room is a stove, with a jug on it. A carriage clock shows the time is precisely nineteen minutes to midnight. On one wall is a portrait of Queen Victoria set within a gold-painted wooden frame. The frame is dusty except for two places about a third of the way down each of its left and right edges. At the far end of the room are three doors, and you surmise that these lead further into the boiler house and the engine rooms.

"Look behind the cabinets," you instruct Watson, having made some deductions. "You'll find some poor fellow has been bundled there after being coshed whilst drinking his cocoa outside."

Watson crouches down. To his amazement, there is indeed an inert body rammed behind the cabinets. He drags the man out and quickly checks him for signs of life. The poor fellow is unconscious, a contusion on the back of his head, and his arm looks broken, one finger still through the handle of his enamel cocoa-mug. While Watson tries to bring him round, you look at the filing cabinets.

One drawer – the one marked "H" – has been pulled slightly open.

Set the Code Wheel's Input Letter to H.

▶ *Turn to the number shown*

SET THE HANDS

You set the clock hands to the position and are disappointed that there's no chime or click to suggest anything has changed. Do you open the door?

▶ *Yes, open the door – Turn to 94*

▶ *No, go back and set the hands again – Turn to 86*

SMOKING YOUR PIPE

You close your eyes, lean back in your chair, and take a long, inspiring pull on your pipe. The blue smoke curls up towards the ceiling.

When you open your eyes, you feel ready to deal with the items on the desk in front of you: a white envelope, a black notebook and a folded, green plan.

▶ *Pick up the white envelope – Turn to 79*

▶ *Pick up the black notebook – Turn to 14*

▶ *Pick up the folded, green plan – Turn to 105*

▶ *Get up and explore the right-hand engine house – Turn to 21*

▶ *Enjoy your pipe and wait until the morning – Turn to 67*

THE GOVERNOR

Watson has been busy trying to loosen the chains that bind the governor. He turns to you and shakes his head.

"There are multiple padlocks," he says, "and many chains. I fear we cannot cut them off, some are too thick even if we could find the right tools. And on top of all that, we'd have to do it carefully because we cannot have Mr Smith fall into the pool while he is still encased, otherwise he'd be sure to drown."

The governor, Mr Smith, nods frantically in agreement of the latter point.

"Mr Smith," you ask, "was there anything you were supposed to be doing tonight? Was there a meeting you were supposed to be attending, or a pressing duty at the gaol?"

"No, sir," he replies. "The only thing I was supposed to be doing tonight was sleeping."

"Very well. I think that must mean that someone wanted to make sure I was not somewhere else. And given that you are here, and knowing the mind of the man behind all this–"

"Professor Moriarty," adds Watson by way of explanation to the governor.

"–that place would be Newgate Gaol. I need to get out. And quickly. Sorry, Mr Smith: we can't free you, but we can get out and arrange to have you rescued, afterwards. Come along, Doctor!"

▶ *Climb up the ladder – Turn to 93*

AN ELEMENTARY CODE

from 78

There is a list of the chemicals on the inside of the door. The bottles are arranged in the same order. Some of the elements sound extraordinarily fanciful to you and you feel as if you know things that even a Victorian consulting detective could not possibly know. How strange.

The list shows: Thorium, Rhenium, Einsteinium, Carbon, Oxygen, Rhenium (again), Tungsten, Iodine, Thorium (again), Nickel, Neon, Molybdenum, and finally Rhenium (again).

Each bottle has a label for its chemical symbol, but they've been left blank. It's an elementary code that you are eager to decipher.

▶ *Turn to the number hidden in the chemicals*

THE WATER-LEVEL LOG

The water-level log contains row after row of detailed measurements taken from the filtering beds. The numbers form neat columns, with variations in the levels slowly rising and falling over the days. Everything is measured and controlled – if the numbers ever got too high, someone let some water out; too low, and more would be retained – so mostly this is a book of calming, unexceptional, unstartling numbers.

As you turn page after page your mind follows the gentle rising and falling of the numbers, and your breathing rises and falls in the same gentle way. Before long your brow is resting on the book and you are peacefully, deeply, but not constructively, asleep.

▶ *Fall asleep – Turn to 20*

A RAISED EYEBROW

You turn the dial, but the safe door remains resolutely shut. Watson raises an eyebrow, but he is a decent chap and says nothing.

▶ *Try again – Turn to 96*

INVENTORY

You thumb through more items from the bundle of documents you found in the safe. One is an inventory and incident report from the foreman.

It describes some tomfoolery by a drunken apprentice involving four small bins that, at the start of the incident, contained respectively:

STOCK			
hooks	5	long bolts	10
wide bolts	8	washers	100

The apprentice repositioned single items from each bin to every one of the others (that is, he took 3 wide bolts from the wide bolt bin and put one into each of the other bins; and did the same with the long bolts, the hooks and the washers). He then set about demonstrating with balances that each of the bin's contents now weighed exactly the same.

This interesting discovery, however, failed to amuse the foreman, who insisted that all the parts be returned to their correct bins. The apprentice was subsequently sent to his lodgings with a thick ear, a shilling docked from his wages, and the instruction to sleep off his need to tamper with the pumping station's inventory.

By the time you've finished reading it, you conclude that this episode has no bearing on your current predicament, but you can't help realize – as perhaps the apprentice had realized, too – that you can accurately calculate the relative weights of all the parts from this inebriated display. Such is the curse of having the mind of the world's finest consulting detective: you process all of the information you consume, all of the time. How heavy is a hook?

▶ *As heavy as 6 wide bolts – Turn to 75*

▶ *As heavy as 6 long bolts – Turn to 58*

12:00

You fold up the green plan, but as you do so you notice there's a stamp on the back indicating that someone at the drawing office had signed this off. There are the initials, "C.D." and a number that looks a lot like a time: "12:00".

▶ *Smoke your pipe – Turn to 38*

(45) MANHANDLED

"Don't worry, Watson," you say encouragingly. "I'm confident that the biggest problem we have is the stoker who is the wrong side of that door." At that moment the boiler house door flies off its hinges and the giant man strides through. He looks ready to treat you and Watson in the same manner as the door.

You turn and run: straight into another of Moriarty's hoodlums, just as big and broad as the stoker. Perhaps you got your inferences from the footprints wrong. You curse yourself for a fool. You know your own methods. Why did you not apply them?

The big men pick each of you up by your respective necks and manhandle you back into the office. They slam the door and you hear them laughing from the other side of it.

▶ *Wait in the office – Turn to 67*

(46) THE DAILY GAZETTE

At first glance the collection of documents found in the safe are just the sort of things one might expect from the business of the pumping station. But you know there is more to what's going on here than meets the eye, so you scan through them quickly and pick one item that looks especially interesting.

It's a page from a six-month-old edition of *The Daily Gazette*, which has some holes punched in it.

Find and identify the missing letters, and then decode them using the Code Wheel. Perhaps then you may need to rearrange them to make a number?

▶ *Turn to the number you have discovered*

The Daily Gazette

Notorious Canary Trainer up before "the Beak"

Aloysius Norbert Wilson of Eversholt Street, London NW was bound over for 12 months at Bow Street Magistrate's Court last night after being charged with drunkenness and lewd behaviour in the Tottenham Court Road. In his defence, Wilson claimed that the death by cat of his favourite bird, Delia, had left him inconsolable and grief had driven him to uncharacteristic behaviour. He asked for 29 other convictions to be taken into account.

The Bogus Laundry Affair

Turn to page 26 to read more about the sensational undoing of the Somers Town coiners.

Fatal Accident

A collision on Tuesday at the junction of Fore Street and Finsbury Pavement has resulted in the unfortunate death of Mister Algernon "Algy" Pope. He was crossing the road when he was struck by an out-of-control hansom. Mister Pope, a book-seller, was recently married to Alice, daughter of Mister Sidney Robert Smith Esq., governor of Newgate Gaol. The unfortunate woman now faces life as a young widow and mother, as she was carrying Mister Pope's unborn child at the time of the tragic accident.

THE PICA RETURNS!

More than 60 years after departing from Plymouth, the fabled HMS *Pica* has finally returned home.

The *Pica*, sister ship to the HMS *Beagle*, was set to accompany the *Beagle* on a survey expedition headed for South America. Unfortunately tragedy struck just a week out of port when extreme weather forced the ships in different directions. No word was heard from the *Pica* or its crew until now.

Not ruined by the storm, the ship continued its journey down the coast of Africa into strange waters at the bottom of the world.

Reverend Jackson Whitehead, the ship's chaplain, kept a diary of the trip and created a series of typographic

Rev. Jackson Whitehead - circa 1850

specimens, made of letterforms, numerals and punctuation marks, based on the animals that he discovered during his travels.

The Irene Adler Institute of Etiquette & Deportment

Ladies! Do you get flustered with your forks when dining out? Worried about how to address an archduke? Uncertain that you alight from vehicular conveyances with sufficient decorum and elegance? Fear that your correspondence is not literate? Fret no more. Sign up to the exclusive Irene Adler Institute and learn how to comport yourself to your social advantage.
By Appointment to the Royal House of Bohemia

Lost & Found

Gentleman's Aluminium Crutch, slightly dented on the lower portion. Left on the Metropolitan Line somewhere between Baker Street and Pinner on the evening of January 5th. Small reward. BOX NO 9877

You run out onto the road and flag down a cab – it's still pre-dawn, but there are always some hopefuls about – and rush to Newgate Gaol. The cab races between dark buildings, clattering through the streets as London tries to sleep. The wheels come skidding to a halt outside the prison and you leap out into a group of people milling around the gate; something is afoot. Among the crowd, you recognize Inspector Lestrade of the Yard.

"Holmes," he says, and you see he looks almost flustered. "Do you know anything about all this?"

"About what aspect of this, exactly?"

Lestrade rubs his face wearily. "The governor of the prison authorized the sudden transfer of prisoner Sebastian Moran – you'll remember who he is, I'm sure – to another prison an hour ago. Except it wasn't really the governor, but someone impersonating him."

You snap your fingers. "Of course! We were too slow, Watson." You turn to Lestrade. "It was Moriarty himself, my dear Inspector, who impersonated the governor, and he did so having trapped me inside the pumping station at Kew Bridge, from where we have just come. If you send your men there, they will find Mr Sidney Smith, the real governor, waiting to be unchained. I think we will return to Baker Street now. It has been a long night."

You hail another cab, this time in a manner more resigned than rushed. Watson sits silently beside you as you ride slowly through the streets of London, each of you contemplating the events of that evening. You did well to escape, but you were not in time to thwart Moriarty's execution of his plan. Moriarty, the Napoleon of Crime, has beaten you because – despite another agent's attempt to guide you – you missed something along the way. You didn't quite follow everything perfectly and imperfection is not good enough for Sherlock Holmes.

THE END

The Daily Gazette

GAOLBREAK FROM NEWGATE

Governor Kidnapped. Disguise! Subterfuge!

SHERLOCK HOLMES RESCUES GOVERNOR

Escaped Prisoner is Danger to Public. World's Greatest Consulting Detective Comes Close to Thwarting Masterful Escape Plan.

Dramatic events unfolded at dawn this morning, as the daring and dastardly plans of the criminal mastermind Professor James Moriarty were successfully enacted, despite the best efforts of consulting detective Mr Sherlock Holmes.

The Napoleon of Crime's audacious scheme allowed his henchman, society sniper Colonel Sebastian Moran (49), languishing in Newgate cells awaiting trial for the murder of Mr Robert Adair, to escape incarceration. Mr Sherlock Holmes, together with his faithful companion Dr Watson, failed to arrive in time to foil the plot.

Some may wonder how Moriarty and Moran managed to slip the grasp of the law and the redoubtable Holmes quite so easily. Why was there no guard on the prison gate? Is there something the British public are not being told?

Misdirection and mummery

First reports suggest the governor of Newgate Gaol, Mr Sidney Smith, was kidnapped and held at Kew Waterworks, allowing Moriarty to assume his persona and serving as a diversion to distract Mr Sherlock Holmes.

Mr Smith was collected by Scotland Yard and is recovering at home.

Dr Watson confessed the difficulties he and Holmes had encountered: "It was an audacious stratagem but one that Holmes saw through almost instantaneously. Moriarty might be a master of disguise, good enough to fool the Newgate Gaol staff, but not Holmes; and the riddles and enigmas with which Moriarty sought to delay and divert us from his true intentions were a bracing workout for the brain but not, as it transpires, insoluble. It was unfortunate that time was always against us, for we really stood no chance of escaping swiftly enough to prevent this from occurring, despite our best efforts."

The Murderous Toff

Colonel Sebastian Moran (Eton, Oxford and the 1st Bangalore Pioneers) served with distinction in the Afghan and the Anglo-Indian Wars, and is a famed big-game hunter and prominent member of the Bagatelle Club. He is allegedly Chief of Staff to Professor Moriarty, with special responsibility for overseeing security and heavy removals.

from 25

48 THE QUEEN'S SECRET SERVICE

You carefully put the torn letter back into your pocket (there's more to that note, you are sure). Enamel mugs hang from hooks beside the stove with its empty cocoa jug. Two hooks are empty. A quick glance through the register book on the desk confirms it: there were two people on duty tonight, the foreman and an engineer.

"This chap is still out cold, Holmes," Watson says from his position on the floor. "But his hand has started twitching in a most peculiar way."

You squat down next to Watson and lift the unconscious man's right arm to inspect his hand. It is too clean to be that of an engineer, and there is a smudge of blue ink on the index finger. So this is the foreman, and the work on the word puzzle was his. Watson is correct: the man is making the smallest of turning motions with his hand, alternating clockwise and anticlockwise. You count them carefully.

You walk towards the portrait of the Queen. Your hands naturally hold the frame about a third of the way down. Just as you had expected, it is easy to lift off the wall.

▶ *Take down the picture – Turn to 96*

49 A PICTURE POSTCARD

from 19, 50

You sit down at the desk and compose your thoughts. You're trapped in the pumping station... but there's never been a time when thinking hasn't solved a problem for you. So, you examine the bundle of documents that you took from the safe and see what else can be discovered. As you sort through the papers, you notice a picture postcard with a square of numbers printed on it.

▶ *Examine the postcard – Turn to 56*

A DISCARDED TICKET

The giant stoker is almost upon you! You dash up the stairs, but stumble and fall. You're not hurt, but as you reach out instinctively to save yourself your hand touches something on the stone step. You discover a discarded train ticket for yesterday's 2:15 afternoon stopping service from Waterloo to Brentford – the ticket has been clipped, so it's been used and is of no obvious value. Nonetheless, you are by your nature a hoarder, so you slip the ticket into your pocket, quickly get back to your feet, and escape through the door.

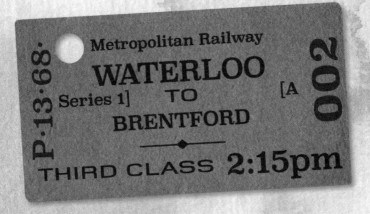

Watson is waiting for you and slams the door as soon as you're through.

▶ *Back in the office – Turn to 49*

A FINAL DOOR

from 27

"Why, Holmes, it's just a child's drawing," Watson cries.

"Oh, that's your idea!" you reply, knowingly. "At first sight it would appear to be some childish prank. It consists of a number of absurd little figures dancing across the floor upon which they are drawn. Why should you attribute any importance to so grotesque an object? In normal circumstance, these hieroglyphics would evidently have a meaning, the object of those who invented the system has apparently been to conceal that these characters convey a message, and to give the idea that they are the mere random sketches of children. Having once recognized, however, that the symbols stood for letters, and having applied the rules that guide us in all forms of secret writings, the solution was easy enough."

Watson hangs on your every word, waiting for you to provide the solution.

"But alas, on this occasion, this is nothing more than another game to keep us incarcerated."

He looks despondent, not that you notice.

You smooth down the corner of the rug.

"Very well, Watson. There is one door we haven't been through yet. That has to be the one that leads to our liberty... although I doubt this is going to be a straightforward exit."

You grasp the handle of the door in the north wall of the office, and try to open the door.

▶ *Open the door – Turn to 72*

ENJOY THE GAME

The message is addressed to you:

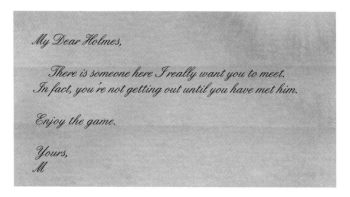

My Dear Holmes,

*There is someone here I really want you to meet.
In fact, you're not getting out until you have met him.*

Enjoy the game.

*Yours,
M*

You are not surprised. Your arch-enemy Moriarty engineered your presence here – you suspected as much already. The only question is whether you are equal to the challenge he has set you. It's clear that there is no "planning meeting" for a Newgate gaolbreak as the note had suggested: that was simply a lie. But something else is going on, and Moriarty is deliberately keeping you here to prevent your interference.

▶ *Take the original letter out of your pocket – Turn to 25*

NO CLICK

You set the clock hands to the position and are disappointed that there's no chime or click to suggest anything has changed.

Do you open the door?

▶ *Yes, open the door – Turn to 13*

▶ *No, go back and set the hands again – Turn to 86*

(54) THE MAUDSLAY ENGINE ROOM

from 91

The great Maudslay beam engine is pitching up and down in its majestic, powerful way. The walls echo to the sound of its mighty work. Fly-wheels turn and great leather belts shudder as they pass. Occasional alarming clangs ring out from somewhere near the lofty ceiling. Puffs of steam drift over the polished floor, giving the engine room the air of a lake on a misty morning.

Watson, ahead of you, is fascinated by the industrial marvel. With his voice barely registering above the sound of the pistons he roars: "Underneath the steam engine, that's what the note said!"

As you move towards it, you already know that there is nothing underneath the Maudslay engine but the foundations to the building. A dead end, or a misunderstood clue?

You try to think if there's anything that you know of the Maudslay that might help, but nothing comes to mind. As you start to examine the engine, could there be some sign as to where you should head next?

▶ *Find your answer and turn to it*

from 24

(55) STEAM

The maze is a little tricky but you don't need to worry about that.
The important thing, as Watson reminds you, is to leave this particular
engine house.

The steam hisses fiercely and you feel its scalding heat against your face as
you pass through it. You leave the engineer where he lies.

▶ *Go back to the office – Turn to 32*

from 49

(56) THE MAGIC SQUARE

Watson looks over your shoulder and nods knowledgeably. "Well, Holmes,
that's what they call a magic square," he says. "Every column and every row
adds up to the same number."

You don't agree or disagree, so he continues.

"And furthermore, that's Dürer's magic square from *Melencolia I*, unless I
am very much mistaken."

He seems surprised by your silence.

"I'm not mistaken am I, Holmes?"

You smile.

"No, Doctor, you are not." He puffs up his chest and is about to say
something when you add: "Except... this one is wrong. Someone has
swapped two of the numbers."

▶ *Add the two misplaced numbers together – Turn to your answer*

12	3	2	13
5	10	11	8
9	6	7	16
4	15	14	1

(57) THE CLOCK HANDS

You set the clock hands to the position and are disappointed that there's no chime or click to suggest anything has changed.

Do you open the door?

▶ *Yes, open the door – Turn to 98*

▶ *No, go back and set the hands again – Turn to 86*

(58) A RED NOTEBOOK

You rifle through the documents and notice a red notebook. Every one of its pages has a page number printed on it, but due to an error at the publisher's every fourth number was skipped in the series.

So, the pages are numbered 1, 2, 3, 5, 6, 7, 9, 10, 11, 13... and so on.

You turn to the twelfth page. It has the number 15 printed there.

There are 32 pages in the book.

What number is printed on the last page?

▶ *An even number – Turn to 88*

▶ *An odd number – Turn to 106*

(59) A PIECE OF PAPER

from 7

You prefer to solve more challenging tasks than word puzzles. They are ultimately unsatisfactory because they are artificial and lack any of the rigour and reality of evidence, data and deduction.

"Have you cracked it, Holmes?" asks Watson looking up from the unconscious man.

Pushing the newspaper aside, you open the folder that you extracted from the drawer marked "H". It contains a single piece of paper with a short message written on it.

▶ *Read the message – Turn to 52*

(60) THE ENTRANCE YARD

from 84, 108

You signal to Watson to step lightly. Both of you slip through the open gate into the entrance yard.

You point towards the front of the main building. The doors are elegant and tall, and a light from inside shines through the fan-light window above them. Watson nods to indicate that he has understood your intention. A hand-cart overloaded with coal has been left beside the doors, which will help conceal you from the watchman should he look over his shoulder towards the building.

Keeping low, you both quickly make your way across the yard.

▶ *Approach the door – Turn to 112*

A COUPLE OF APES

You run and stumble along the gloomy tunnel as fast as you dare. In the distance you can see the thinnest crack of light, almost impossibly far away at the river-end of the tunnel.

Your feet are snagged and deflected by the uneven sleepers of what was once the hand-cart track. It's difficult progress, but grunts of pursuit echo from the mouth of the tunnel behind you, so you cannot afford to be careful. When you run, you trip and stagger; you end up scurrying forward in a stooped crouch like a couple of apes, hands extended. It's almost impossible to be as fast as you need to be, and when you're about halfway along the infernal tunnel you stop to compose yourselves.

Watson puts his revolver back into his jacket pocket as you pull out a tin of matches. You contemplate if the benefit is going to outweigh the risk; you may be able to progress faster if you can see the ground better ahead of you, but perhaps a light will make you a pin-point target for your enemies should any be armed with a gun. You opt for a middle way: just the flare of a struck match to see what's ahead, and then you'll blow it out.

▶ *Strike the match – Turn to 16*

(62) TORN PIECES

from 79

You put the torn pieces back into their envelope. It's all very well doing puzzles like this – clearly you find them easy – but it's not obvious how it's helping you get out of your current predicament of being trapped in the pumping station. On the other hand, not solving the puzzles certainly won't improve the situation.

► *Smoke your pipe – Turn to 38*

(63) A CRACKED SAFE

from 96

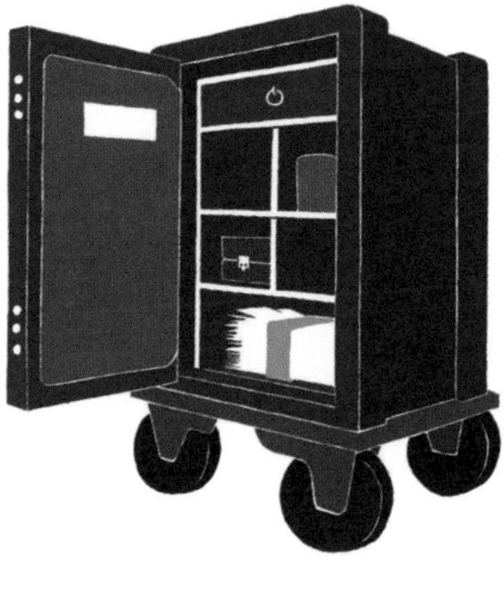

The safe wheel retracts its bolts, and you swing its heavy door open. Inside is a bundle of documents. You lift them out and take them to the table.

► *Sit down and look through the documents – Turn to 46*

(64) NAMES IN A GRID

The last page of the notebook has a grid of letters on it.

You quickly spot names in the grid that are spelled out in straight lines: forwards, backwards, down or up, even diagonally (but always in a straight line; no bending).

Nagging away at everything you see in your current imprisoned state – and perhaps even outside of it – is the invisible hand of your adversary, the Napoleon of Crime, the spider at the centre of the underworld web.

Is the name Moriarty concealed in the grid?

▶ *Yes, Moriarty is in the grid – Turn to 33*

▶ *No, Moriarty is not in the grid – Turn to 74*

NOTES OF NAMES

....

....

....

....

....

....

....

```
E N F Y T R A M R S H U D S O N A O M
P A O F Q E O R M H I R O M Z C I R Y
M R Y S X L A T L E S T R A D E G M N
A O L A T D E M O R I Y K M B W R S O
R M V B C A D I A L A N G D A L E T S
Y N E I G E W Y T O P T R P Y X G E N
M A R L H N E H F C R I A U N B S I H
O I S L Y E Y V N K S O K R E M O N O
R T M Y C R O F T H O L M E S Y N S J
S S L O T I A N I O O M I R I A R T L
T A G H R R T R T L B J O C N D V A L
A B E T U I S H Y M R W I L H E L M E
N E H D O Y L E E E O L A I P X A F W
I S K M H B R A D S T R E E T I E O N
Q U L K W J Y R Q S R A L U G E R R I
W I G G I N S O J A M E S M D O D D H
R A C H E M A T H E L N E Y J O N E S
S O M R S W A R R E N M O I A R T O Z
S R T Y B A K E R E I C H E N B A C H
```

A LUCKY BULLET

No sooner have you confidently declared the number of trained killers at your enemy's disposal than a shot booms out from behind you: one of them is shooting down the tunnel. You hear the bullet ricocheting off the brickwork as it hurtles past you.

You're already over two-thirds of the way along the tunnel so it would have to be an improbably lucky shot to hit you. But such logic has never been a reassurance to all those who have subsequently been struck by such an unlikely bullet. So, you and Watson break into a shambling run. Stumbling, arms outstretched, you hurtle onwards until you hit the end: thin, plain doors chained on the outside against vagabonds.

Watson, slightly ahead of you, does not slow down. His final charge has a spirit of which his former regiment (not to mention rugby club) would have been proud. The doors fly apart, metalwork tearing out of splintered wood, and you see pre-dawn light reflecting off the river water below.

Angry shouts echo down the tunnel behind you, together with one or two more shots, as you dart out of the mouth of the tunnel and turn abruptly left. You run along the river path and past tied-up boats. Scrambling up a flight of stone stairs, you are on Kew Bridge.

Only then do you pause to look behind. Your pursuers know they have been defeated; you see them standing by the broken tunnel doors by the river, looking up at you before slinking back into the hole.

▶ *Hurry to Newgate Gaol... – Turn to 47*

A SEQUENCE OF TIMES

You are back before the door that, were it to open, would let you out of the boiler house and into the grounds of the pumping station – and thereby, presumably, freedom.

Watson stands beside you, and once again the two of you look at the wires, flasks and mechanisms of the booby-trap that stands between you and escape. There's a clock-face on it, with hands that you can reposition. You have concluded that you just need to set those hands to a specific time to disarm the trap and allow you to harmlessly open the door.

"Do you know what time to set it to?" asks Watson, in a manner that is as predictable as it is infuriating.

Of course you know what time to set it to – don't you? But because you know he's at heart a very good sort – in fact, the very best of sorts – you indulge Watson with an explanation.

"I've already got a collection of precise times I have carefully observed," you say. "So I just need to identify the pattern that binds them. Then, the time I need will be the missing one in that arrangement."

"I see," says Watson, although you both know that he probably doesn't. "So... what time is that?"

You prepare to set the hands on the clock-face of the booby-trapped contraption to the required time.

▶ *Set the hands on the clock-face – Turn to 86*

IMPLICATED

from 6, 13, 20, 21, 33, 38, 45, 77, 85, 94, 98, 111

You resign yourself to being stuck in the pumping station, and light your pipe once more. If only you had your violin with you; a few bars of Mendelssohn may have driven away the stench of failure for a time. Watson gazes glumly out of the window, and you both await rescue.

As the sun rises, the new shift arrives at the pumping station. The coal is shovelled away from the front door and men make their way into the engine rooms. The place is a crime scene – the engineer is dead in one of the engine rooms and the governor of Newgate Gaol is chained up in the other – and waiting in the midst of it all is you, Sherlock Holmes, and your uncomfortable assistant Doctor Watson.

The policeman who confronts you, perhaps inevitably, is Inspector Lestrade of Scotland Yard.

"Did you know a prisoner was released by the governor at Newgate last night? Except we now know it wasn't really the governor, who all this time was imprisoned here with you..."

His expression is a mix of distaste and disappointment.

"I think you should go home, Holmes. You can expect us to have some questions for you later."

You make your way wearily back to 221B Baker Street. As your hansom pulls up outside the door, you see a small group of reporters waiting to greet you. They surge forward as you step down from the cab.

THE END

The Daily Gazette

GAOLBREAK FROM NEWGATE
Governor Kidnapped.
Disguise! Subterfuge!
SHERLOCK HOLMES IMPLICATED
Escaped Prisoner is Danger to Public. World's Greatest Consulting Detective Yet To Explain Involvement In Escape Plan.

Alarm and despondency struck at Newgate early this morning as Professor James Moriarty, the Napoleon of Crime, successfully sprang his murderous henchman, Colonel Sebastian Moran, from gaol in a spectacular and audacious plot. Not only did he make a fool of the full force of the law, he also baffled and outfoxed the self-styled Greatest Consulting Detective in the country, Mr Sherlock Holmes.

According to Inspector G. Lestrade, Moriarty kidnapped the real Governor, Mr Sidney Smith (who is thought to be innocent of any collusion), and imprisoned him at the Kew Pumping Station. Disguising himself as Smith, the Professor authorized the transfer of prisoner Moran to another gaol. In reality, both have vanished like Scotch mist. And the great British public will not sleep easy in their homes.

Humiliation and Ignominy for Holmes

Professor Moriarty was evidently confident he could elude the long arm of the law as he has done so often before, and contrived an elaborate plot to lure his arch-enemy, Sherlock Holmes, away from the scene of the daring escape. The Professor need not have bothered; Holmes failed to deduce his way through the fiendish enigmas and conundrums, got himself and Watson trapped in the Pumping Station and was forced to wait in shameful ignominy until rescued, along with the noble Mr Smith.

Thanks to Holmes' disgraceful ineptitude, an arch-criminal and a murderous fiend are on the loose, thumbing their noses at the rule of law. One is forced to conclude that either Holmes has lost all his cognitive powers or, more sinister still, that he is in covert partnership with Moriarty and both are plotting the overthrow of society.

The Murderous Toff

Colonel Sebastian Moran (Eton, Oxford and the 1st Bangalore Pioneers) served with distinction in the Afghan and the Anglo-Indian Wars, and is a famed big-game hunter and prominent member of the Bagatelle Club. Colonel Moran is allegedly Chief of Staff to Professor Moriarty, with special responsibility for security and removals.

(68) ALL THE ONES

from 14

You are making progress – solving puzzles is always progress – but you wonder how you're doing for time. You flip open your pocket watch. Either your watch is wrong or it's getting late: all the ones, eleven minutes past one in the morning.

▶ *Smoke your pipe – Turn to 38*

(69) A SECRET DRAWER

from 40

Your cogitation is interrupted by the noise of the stoker slamming the cast-iron door shut on the firebox he's been feeding. You hear his heavy boots walking in your direction.

"I think we should go back into the office," says Watson.

Before you depart, you run your fingers along the underside of the shelf. Your suspicions are correct – there's a hidden drawer, and you slide it open. It's empty, but you notice a pattern has been scratched into the base. You pull the drawer all the way out so you can inspect it more clearly.

▶ *Examine the pattern – Turn to 22*

A BURST OF INSPIRATION

from 24

As you quickly solve the maze, a sudden thought occurs to you. Returning to the torn note (1) that you were handed at the start of the night, perhaps you should look at all the letters that have a nick above them.

On its own, the clue might not seem to make any sense, but maybe it's part of a larger puzzle? You stroke your chin thoughtfully.

The hissing steam reminds you that you need to get out of here. You leave the engineer where he lies.

▶ *Go back to the office – Turn to 32*

A BLOODY FOOTPRINT

from 54

Cast-iron stairs lead up to another floor, where the engine beam itself rocks up and down. Spotting something up there, you ascend the stairs. At the top you find evidence of what you had suspected: an oily rag draped over the iron railing on the metal walkway, an enamel jug beside it and half a mug of cold cocoa. Engineers don't leave mugs on their machines unless they have been interrupted. You lean over and look down.

From up here you can see someone below, beside the engine. It's a cramped location, obscured from your earlier position when you came into the room. You walked right past them without even noticing. The person you see is sitting, legs outstretched, propped up against an upright pipe. The blood on the floor tells you this is not someone resting. You have found another body – and judging by the amount of scarlet, this time it's unlikely to be one Watson can hope to revive.

You rattle back down the staircase and approach the engineer – for that is clearly who it is. His head is flopped forward, his chin on his chest. The pattern of blood on the floor starts with splashes by the base of the machine he had been tending, followed by smeared splatters where he was dragged, to be left slumped against the wall where the last of the blood forms a pool.

There is a single footprint in the blood. You are more than familiar with observing the characteristics of a footprint at the scene of the crime, so you tell Watson to make a mental note of this one: a square-toed boot of someone's left foot, with a nail missing halfway down the outside edge, and worn at the inside of the heel.

▶ *Examine the engineer – Turn to 100*

THE BOILER HOUSE

You step through the door into a large hall. It contains several large boilers, with furnaces and crates of coal. On the far side is a door that, if your instincts are correct, opens to the outside. Steps lead down to the boiler house floor.

You deduce from noises beyond the regular wheeze of the waterworks' engines that there is someone working here. As you wait on the steps, observing your surroundings, a giant of a man, carrying an equally enormous shovel, steps out from between the boilers. A red kerchief is tied around his neck, which is not unlike that of a prize bull. He hasn't spotted you yet, and you might be able to use this to your advantage. His presence does not distract your keen eye from the figure of a Dancing Man scratched into the wall, which seems to be signalling to you...

▶ *Turn to the hidden number*

A PAUSE FOR THOUGHT

You stuff the pieces of the blueprint back into the envelope, and extinguish your pipe. The handwritten note on the envelope matched the layout on the blueprint, but the events of this evening have knocked you off your stride. To your unfathomable exasperation, you got the puzzle wrong. You crave a little of your favourite seven-per-cent solution, although you know Watson would fiercely disapprove. You don't normally bother with sleep, but maybe you should clear your head with a little nap.

▶ *You fall asleep – Turn to 20*

THE CLOCKMAKER'S CONUNDRUM

You push the notepad away and look over to the carriage clock. There's a piece of folded paper tucked under the base. When you point it out, Watson brings it to you at the desk. You unfold the paper, flatten it out, and read the printed text. It's a puzzle about a time:

```
Start at 10:30. Find the
next time the hour hand
and the minute hand are
in exactly a straight
line pointing away from
each other. Two hours
before that.
```

Round the time down to hours and minutes (don't worry about the seconds).

▶ *When you've solved the puzzle – Turn to 89*

(75) TWO BOOKS

You push the inventory report aside and look for more interesting diversions. In a drawer in the desk, there are two books.

One is the foreman's diary, containing excruciating detail of the hours he has worked over the last several months. The other is a logbook containing hundreds of recorded water-levels from the filtering beds through which the London pumping station's water is passed.

▶ *Read the foreman's diary – Turn to 34*

▶ *Analyse the logbook – Turn to 41*

A PRECISE TIME

You ask the governor how he came to be chained to the wall above the suction pool, while Watson investigates the chains that are wound about his arms, legs and body.

"I had finished my office at around six this evening," replies Smith, "and returned to my house for dinner. Just as I was sitting down at the table to eat, two ruffians came from out of nowhere to apprehend me..."

You interrupt brusquely: "What time was that, Mr Smith?"

"Well, I suppose... You mean, the precise time?"

"Precise is always best. And you are precise in your habits, are you not?"

"I am, sir. It would have been 7:03pm."

"Thank you. Carry on."

The governor resumes his tale: "I was sitting down to eat, as I said, and they suddenly appeared, with arms drawn, and a sack to put over my head. They carried me here and chained me to the wall. The last thing they said before shutting that trapdoor and leaving me in the dark here was: 'Mr Sherlock Holmes will be along to find you... if he is clever enough.'"

He pauses, but you say nothing. So he goes on.

"Well it seems they were right: you were clever enough. Thank you."

As you take out the letter you were sent, to show the governor, you suddenly realize that there is another number hidden in the coded note. You check all the letters on pink paper.

▶ *Turn to the number described by letters on pink paper*

OUTNUMBERED

No sooner have you confidently declared the number of trained killers at your enemy's disposal than a shot booms out from behind you: one of them is shooting into the tunnel. You hear the bullet ricochet off the brickwork as it speeds past you.

You're already a long way down the tunnel, so it would have to be an improbably lucky shot to hit you… but that's never been a reassurance to all those who have been struck by such luck. So, you and Watson break into a shambling run. Stumbling, arms outstretched, you hurtle onwards until you hit the end: thin, plain doors chained on the outside against vagabonds. Watson, slightly ahead of you, does not slow down. His final charge has a spirit of which his former regiment (not to mention rugby club) would have been proud, but the chains hold and he bounces back, defeated.

You turn to see your pursuers striding purposefully down the tunnel to get you. You are outnumbered by armed men.

They bundle you both back up the tunnel. You are roughly marched back to the office, where – seemingly to the amusement of the ruffians who are imprisoning you – you will be obliged to wait until dawn.

At least you have not been shot. And they let you keep your pipe.

▶ *Wait in the office – Turn to 67*

(78) A CURIOUS CABINET

As you walk back through the boiler house, you look over to the giant stoker, standing by the open firebox of the furnace he had been feeding. He is leaning on his shovel watching you, and he still has the slightest of smiles playing across his otherwise impassive slab of a face.

Before you reach the steps back up to the office, you notice the chemicals in the cabinet once more. Something very odd about the labels demands your attention. After all, you're something of a scientist yourself – the chemistry bench back at your lodgings in Baker Street affords endless hours of diversion and distraction in the intolerably tedious lulls between cases.

You can't resist looking at the labels more closely. Watson stops and looks too. He's not unfamiliar with chemicals himself, being a medical man, but he doesn't share your knack for spotting patterns and hidden codes.

▶ *Examine the bottles – Turn to 40*

A BLUEPRINT

The white envelope has a handwritten legend written upon on it:

1 = Y, 4 = W, and 5 = T ?

Inside, you find five pieces of a blueprint showing water pipes. It's been torn up, but it's not too difficult for you to rearrange the pieces.

Clearly the handwriting on the envelope is describing pipe routes on that blueprint... but the letters on the blueprint are A through to E. Perhaps the letters on the blueprint need to be encoded using the Code Wheel to match the note.

Follow the number on the blueprint to its corresponding letter.

Then use the Code Wheel to decode the letter.

1 = ☐ = ☐

4 = ☐ = ☐

5 = ☐ = ☐

Does your answer match the writing on the envelope?

▶ *Yes – Turn to 62*

▶ *No – Turn to 73*

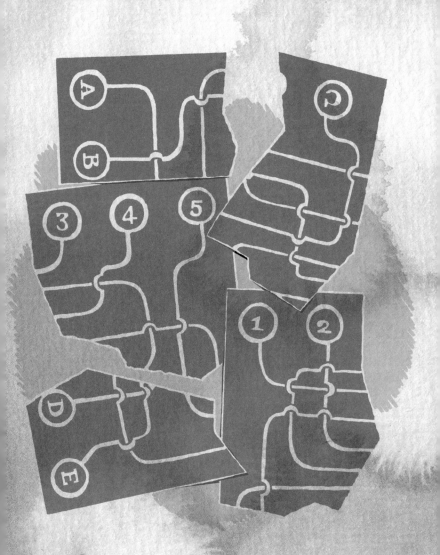

A NUMBER OF HOODLUMS

The noise of your pursuers echoes down the tunnel. The uneven and debris-strewn ground impedes the hunters as well the hunted. But the scurrying of rats disrupt your concentration.

"How many killers does Moriarty have at his disposal?" pants Watson.

"It's an interesting question, Watson," you reply, with irritating calm. "My Irregulars have over the years gathered some very specific information about his operation, and I can tell you this. Moriarty teaches the hoodlums in his inner circle four distinct methods of killing: poisoning, marksmanship, strangulation and knife-work. Every hoodlum in his inner circle knows exactly two of those methods."

"That seems... oddly specific," says the doctor.

"Moriarty is a professor of mathematics, Watson, so he cannot help himself. But it is that weakness which allows us to calculate the number of hoodlums in his inner circle. Because – and this, my dear friend, is the key – he also ensures that, whichever pair of methods you pick, there will be one and only one hoodlum who is trained in them both."

Watson stops and thinks for a moment, and then shakes his head.

"Holmes could you stop being so ineffably infuriating and tell me roughly how many of these hoodlums he has?"

▶ *"Fewer than 7" – Turn to 83*

▶ *"More than 7" – Turn to 77*

LITTLE DRUMMOND STREET

We arrived at Little Drummond Street – a rather sordid little thoroughfare right on the edge of the notorious Somers Town.

"Come Watson," cried Holmes, springing from the cab. "I have an inkling that Sir Pumfrey is about to emblazon me on a £5 note."

Inside the building, there was a small counter presided over by a thin and very clean-looking young girl. "Watson, explain your predicament," murmured Holmes, beaming at her. "Distract her. You are the ladies' man."

I began to explain about the wrong collars and felt quite caddish as she wilted in front of me like blanched celery. Holmes meanwhile was poking around with his riding crop, hoiking bags of laundry aside and working his way to the curtained entrance leading to the business end of the establishment. The poor little waif was shaking with fear.

"Begging your pardon, sir, but customers ain't allowed in the laundry room, sir, Mrs Rastroy will be ever so cross."

Blithely ignoring her, Holmes plunged on with me right behind him. Steam assailed us, together with an overwhelming smell of hot linen and carbolic. Holmes strode along between the mangles and bench wringers and great copper vats full of boiling bedlinen tended by tiny, bleached wretches wielding long, wooden ladles. He was behaving dashed oddly, even by his own unfathomable standards, capering about and banging on the floor with his crop, and occasionally stopping to bounce up and down on the spot. I could not hear myself think for the hiss of steam, but Holmes persisted, beating a strangely repetitive rhythm, "Dah dah dit, dit dit, dit dah dit dit, dit dah dit dit."

Suddenly the great boiler fell silent, having reached a temperature with which it felt temporarily satisfied. Holmes rapped out his jig once again, then bent towards the floor and listened intently. "D'ye hear that, Watson?"

▶ *Turn to 109*

A GRATEFUL LONDON

You run out onto the road and, flagging down a hansom on Kew Bridge, rush to Newgate Gaol.

The cab races between dark buildings, clattering through the streets as London tries to sleep. The wheels skitter on the stones as you skid to a halt outside the prison gates. There is another carriage – a two-horse Clarence – standing by the gates with its driver sitting ready and its door swung open, and a broad, neckless man with a bald head loitering beside it. You are not too late! Leaving Watson to pay off your hansom, you spring down and run towards the prison door.

The door swings open before you have covered half the distance. A guard appears momentarily to survey the scene before a top-hatted gentleman with grey mutton-chop whiskers and a silver-tipped cane steps confidently through. Behind him, in the dimly lit courtyard, you glimpse a prisoner being led by more guards. "Stop!" you cry. "This is not the governor!"

There is a shout and a sudden report as a gun goes off behind you. You spin round in time to see Watson wrestle the bald man by the Clarence down to the ground, as a snub-nosed pistol clatters away over the cobbles – the doctor having knocked his aim aside even as the shot was fired at you. The guards in the courtyard bundle the prisoner into a corner and quickly make him secure, while two more run out with cudgels drawn. The carriage driver slaps his reins and the carriage lurches off, its open door flapping. The guards pull apart the two fighting men – Watson and the gunman – and hold them both even as the carriage disappears into the night. Another guard throws his weight against the prison door and it swings shut.

You look down. At your feet is a silver-tipped cane and one half of a pair of fake mutton-chop sideburns. You've stopped Sebastian Moran from being sprung from the gaol... but the false governor, Moriarty, has disappeared.

▶ *The following afternoon... – Turn to 92*

The Daily Gazette

GAOLBREAK FROM NEWGATE

Governor Kidnapped. Disguise! Subterfuge!

SHERLOCK HOLMES SAVES THE DAY

World's Greatest Consulting Detective Arrives In Nick Of Time. Dangerous Criminal Remains Behind Bars While A Grateful London Celebrates.

There were triumphant scenes at Newgate early this morning, as Inspector Lestrade of Scotland Yard foiled the plans of fiendish Professor James Moriarty, self-styled Napoleon of Crime, and his homicidal henchman, Colonel Sebastian Moran. Our streets are safe once more and the most powerful criminal web ever spun has been irretrievably ripped apart.

The sun was only just rising when Lestrade and his men, alerted by the great Consulting Detective Sherlock Holmes and his companion Dr Watson, pounced. Moriarty, disguised as the gaol governor Sidney Smith, had newly authorized the 'transfer' of his dastardly co-fiend Moran, but just as both felons were clambering into their respective conveyances, Lestrade gave the order: warders and constables swooped and swiftly prevented Moran's escape. Society may be safe from Moran for the time being, however the mastermind himself escaped; tearing off his false whiskers and discarding his trick paunch, he fled the scene in a high-powered two-horse carriage. Some may wonder how Moriarty managed to slip the grasp of the law and the redoubtable Holmes quite so easily.

Heroic Holmes

Although Dr Watson, forever the soldier, helped subdue one of Moriarty's henchmen, Holmes stood by and allowed Lestrade to take the credit. "It was a simple matter for me," Holmes said modestly. "Moriarty has always had a fatal penchant for the blindingly obvious. I deduced his plan almost immediately, but to provide a false sense of security – and to allow Lestrade the kudos of catching Moran red-handed – we let the game run its course. It was a most bracing exercise for brain and body," he laughed.

Inspector Lestrade thanked Sherlock Holmes and Dr Watson for their help and invaluable support.

The Murderous Toff

Colonel Sebastian Moran (Eton, Oxford and the 1st Bangalore Pioneers) served with distinction in the Afghan and the Anglo-Indian Wars, and is a famed big-game hunter and prominent member of the Bagatelle Club. He is allegedly Chief of Staff to Professor Moriarty, with special responsibility for overseeing security and undertaking heavy removals.

A RUGBY CHARGE

No sooner have you confidently declared the number of trained killers at your enemy's disposal than a shot booms out from behind you: one of them is shooting into the tunnel. You hear the bullet ricochet off the brickwork as it hurtles past you.

You're already a long way down the tunnel, so it would have to be an improbably lucky shot to hit you... but that's never been a reassurance to all those who have been struck by such luck. So, you and Watson break into a shambling run – stumbling, arms outstretched, you hurtle onwards until you hit the end: thin, plain doors chained on the outside against vagabonds.

Watson, slightly ahead of you, does not slow down. His final charge has a spirit of which his former regiment (not to mention rugby club) would have been proud. The doors fly apart, metalwork splintering out of the planks, and you see pre-dawn light reflecting off the river water below.

Angry shouts echo down the tunnel behind you, together with one or two more shots, as you dart out of the mouth of the tunnel and turn abruptly left. You run along the river path and past tied-up boats. Scrambling up a flight of stone stairs, you are on Kew Bridge.

Only then do you pause to look behind you. Your pursuers know they have been defeated; you see them standing by the broken tunnel doors by the river, looking up at you before slinking back into the hole.

▶ *And finally... – Turn to 82*

AN UNEXPECTED OPENING

You walk alongside the railings until you come to the gates of the Grand Junction Waterworks pumping station. This is the place that, day and night, pushes water out to other parts of London, urging it through reservoirs and filter beds, providing a supply that drips, sloshes or gushes from standpipes and house-taps in places as far apart as Ealing, Paddington and beyond.

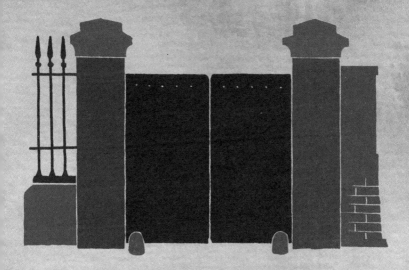

A little brazier glows near the entrance at the foot of the tower, and as you look through the railings you see the door open. A watchman appears, a heavy coat over his shoulders. He steps out of the door and up to the brazier. Turning his back to you, he warms his hands above the fire. The gates in front of you have been, surprisingly, left ajar.

▶ *Dither by the gates – Turn to 108*

▶ *Go through the gates – Turn to 60*

▶ *Look for an alternative entrance – Turn to 5*

EXPLOSION

Just as you finish your calculations, the glass in one of the valves shatters.
Moments later, steam begins to jet out of one of the pipes. Perhaps the
increasing pitch of the hissing means other things are about to break.
If your numbers are correct, the engine is running at the correct pressure.
If, however, you are in error, then you might be in grave danger.

You start over from the beginning, but there just isn't enough time. What
started as a low rumbling is now a mighty roar and the pistons are operating
far faster than they were ever intended to. You stand frozen to the spot,
waiting for the inevitable. But, at the very last moment, Watson pulls you
behind a pillar.

The beam engine explodes.

You are shaken, but uninjured. Debris from the explosion is strewn across
the room, and has blocked the only door in and out. There's little more you
can do but wait for some assistance.

▶ *Wait for help – Turn to 67*

SETTING THE HANDS

Watson seems a little nervous as you reach forward and set the clock hands to
the time you've confidently determined is the setting that will disarm the trap.

▶ *Set the clock hands to 12:00 – Turn to 57*

▶ *Set the clock hands to 2:21 – Turn to 53*

▶ *Set the clock hands to 3:22 – Turn to 37*

▶ *Set the clock hands to 4:39 – Turn to 30*

A CLEFT HEEL

As you make your way across the boiler house floor again, you see that the stoker is working the firebox of another boiler. He's been moving around, and you see the footprints he's left in the coal dust. You pause to look at them carefully: he's got a cleft in the left boot's heel and a hole in the sole – which leaves a distinctive mark.

As you stand studying the prints, you notice that the sound of shovelling has stopped. You stand upright and see that the stoker is also standing erect, staring at you silently. He's some distance away but somehow that doesn't make him any less intimidating. You hurry on towards the door, and its booby-trapped contraption.

▶ *Go to the door – Turn to 66*

A SLOW CLOCK

You are distracted from your investigation of the page numbers by Watson snapping his pocket-watch shut. The look on his face suggests he's just used it to make a discovery. The importance of that discovery remains to be seen and presumably depends on you.

"The clock here is running ten minutes slow," Watson declares.

You don't doubt your companion's observation, but your habit is always to instinctively check such assertions. So you pull out your own watch and flip it open. It is indeed as the doctor has claimed. The carriage clock you noticed when you first came into the office is showing a time that is precisely wrong by 10 minutes.

▶ *Look at the last page of the red notebook – Turn to 64*

Turn to 64

A PLAN OF THE PUMPING STATION

As you finish noting your answer in your pocket notebook, Watson makes an announcement.

"There's something on the back of the Queen."

It seems an odd and intimate thing to mention, but then you realize he means the back of the portrait of the Queen. You lifted it off the wall to access the safe, but hadn't looked at the painting itself.

Watson passes it over to you and you lay it out, face-down (no disrespect intended to Her Majesty) and look at what appears to be a floor plan.

"It's a plan of the pumping station," says Watson.

Indeed it is. And it shows something neither of you knew about before: there's a coal tunnel that runs from the yard which the booby-trapped door opens onto, under the fence and the gates, and out to the river.

"That might be very helpful," you say.

► *"I think it's time we left"* – Turn to 31

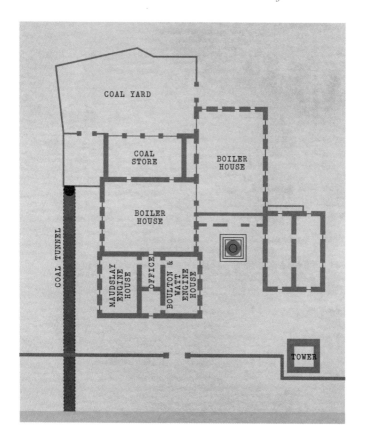

BOULTON & WATT ENGINE ROOM

You go out through the right-hand door, into the Boulton & Watt engine room. The engine is plunging up and down with its powerful strokes. You can hear the sound of the water being drawn up from the suction pool beneath the chequer-plate floor and sent surging on its way through the heavy pipes.

From the top of the steps, you suffer a sudden rush of vertigo and a sense that you're not standing at the top of some water pipes but on the brink of a vertiginous waterfall.

Recovering yourself, you clamber down the steps and notice the hieroglyphs of Dancing Men scratched here and there into the metalwork. Taking out your magnifying glass you can see them clearly enough to decode their semaphore message.

Use the Code Wheel to decipher the Dancing Men.

▶ *Turn to the number you discover*

MORIARTY'S TAUNT

from 15

"HAVE YOU FOUND THE GOVERNOR YET BELOW THE STEAM ENGINE?" Moriarty is taunting you.

Watson interrupts your thoughts. "He's still out cold, the poor devil," he says. "I haven't got anything on me to help revive him."

"I fear there will be at least one more person – possibly two people – who might need your help, Watson. Come!"

And with that you spring up from your chair and hurry out through the left-hand door into one of the engine rooms.

▶ *Enter the Maudslay engine room – Turn to 54*

221B BAKER STREET

from 82

Mrs Hudson places the tray on the table between you. She's brought tea for you and your guests, Mr Sidney Robert Smith, governor of Newgate Gaol, and his daughter Alice. The governor has come here to thank you and Doctor Watson for precipitating his rescue the day before, and for having disrupted the attempted escape of Newgate inmate and Moriarty's henchman Colonel Sebastian Moran.

Mr Smith shakes you warmly by the hand. "It is fortunate indeed that you figured it all out, Mr Holmes," he says. He goes on to describe how he came to be kidnapped by men he now knows to have been Moriarty's lackeys, and used as bait to distract you from the real crime.

Watson listens intently but your mind wanders, because you have already inferred all the important details from the events that have transpired. You look instead to his daughter, Alice, a quiet but alert young woman – widowed tragically young, as you had deduced before you met, and confirmed here by an entirely unscratched wedding band on her digitus quartus.

Despite her silence you know Alice to be sharp-witted, as evidenced by pencil marks on the back of a pocketbook she carries along with her parasol; jottings that you recognize as workings around the word 'denouement', which was the trickiest part of the word puzzle in this morning's edition of *The Times*.

"I trust your baby is back in your safekeeping, and is well," you say to the young woman, who nods gratefully in reply. Watson seems surprised that you knew she had a baby, but, unlike you, he is not remembering back to the unequal couple standing under the gaslight at the beginning of this whole affair, and the bundle being held by the hoodlum who was accompanying her. "And thank you for tampering with the note that Moriarty forced you to deliver to me."

"I was so afeared for my baby, and my father," Alice replies shyly, "that I could not risk direct communication. I had to play my part. But I was confident that the great Sherlock Holmes would require only the subtlest of clues; so I was emboldened enough to dare communicate them to you in the form of a code, sir, despite the risk."

"It... it was you who delivered the torn note?" Watson asks her, catching up. He is the dearest of fellows, but incredibly slow sometimes. And he always goes to chivalrous pieces in the presence of the fairer sex.

You lift your teacup to your lips, and close your eyes, savouring the taste of Mrs Hudson's excellent tea.

THE END

EXASPERATION

You leave the trapdoor open so that the governor at least has some light. Doctor Watson has found the governor's pewter hip-flask in the captive's pocket, and administers a courage-inspiring draft to the poor man before following you up the ladder. There's no way out of the Boulton & Watt engine room except back through the office, so you return there.

"Watson, we need to get out of here quickly."

"Well... yes," replies the doctor, and you can't help but notice a tone of exasperation in your loyal companion's voice as you sit back down at the desk. Was that an involuntary roll of the eye you detected?

"I need to find the time to which we set the clock-hands on the contraption on the booby-trapped door. When that is disarmed, we can leave."

"What about that giant fellow with the shovel in the boiler house?"

"I think he is not a problem we need to solve," you reply. "If he was trying to kill us, he would have done better than just look amused at our finding the way out is booby-trapped. No, my dear doctor, we are being contained, not killed. I intend to escape."

▶ *Look at more documents from the safe – Turn to 43*

AN EXPLOSION

Although you had expected to fling open the door and jump through, a weight has been added to the outside, and the hinges have been stiffened so that it won't be opened quickly. As you push on the door, you see the wires and cogs of the contraption tug away at stoppers and tip up the flasks.

"Get away from it!" cries Watson as he jumps clear. You follow suit, leaping back and away from it.

The contraption explodes and sends debris and billowing smoke towards you. You're thrown to the floor by the blast. Almost immediately there's the impact of the door slamming shut again, and the tinkle of fragments of glass and metal bouncing off the metal boilers. When everything is quiet, you hear the giant stoker begin to laugh.

You and Watson both get to your feet and stagger back to the office.

▶ *In the office – Turn to 67*

FOLDED

You fold up the green plan.

▶ *Smoke your pipe – Turn to 38*

THE CODE OF THE FOREMAN'S HAND

You lift the portrait of the Queen from the wall to reveal a safe. A cast-iron plaque on the front declares it to be a product of the Withy Grove Stores safe company, which happens to be one of several types with which you are familiar. So, you know the wheel will make a satisfying click as you spin it through the correct pattern of turns. You expect the right sequence to be the one you've just read from the movements of the foreman's hand.

Start by turning the Code Wheel to Input Letter X (check this reveals the number 6).

FIRST: Turn the dial anticlockwise 6 places.

SECOND: Note the number shown on the dial at the end of that first move. Turn the dial clockwise as many places as shown by that number.

THIRD: Note the new number. Turn the dial anticlockwise as many places as shown by that number.

FOURTH: Turn the dial clockwise the number of places shown by the number at the end of the third move.

You are finally in position.

Carefully note the Output Letter (there are instructions at the front of the Escape Book, if you are unsure).

Now turn the Code Wheel so that the Input Letter window shows that letter.

What colour is shown in the Code Wheel?

▶ *Green – Turn to 42*

▶ *Yellow – Turn to 35*

▶ *Blue – Turn to 63*

(97) A SHORT MESSAGE

That's the trouble with word puzzles. They are ultimately unsatisfactory because they are artificial and lack any of the rigour and reality of evidence, data and deduction.

"Have you solved it, Holmes?" asks Watson looking up from the unconscious man and raising his eyebrows at your peeved expression.

Pushing the newspaper aside, you open the folder that you took out of the drawer marked "H". It contains a single piece of paper with a short message written up on it.

▶ *Read the message – Turn to 52*

(98) A HEAVY DOOR

Although you had expected to fling the door open and jump through, a weight has been added to the outside, and the hinges have been stiffened so it won't be opened quickly. As you push on it you see the wires and cogs of the contraption tug away at stoppers and tip up the flasks.

"Get away from it!" cries Watson as he jumps clear. You follow suit, leaping back and away from it.

The contraption explodes and sends debris and billowing smoke towards you. You're thrown onto the floor by the blast. Almost immediately there's the impact of the door slamming shut again, and the tinkle of fragments of glass and metal bouncing off the metal boilers. When everything is quiet, you hear the giant stoker begin to laugh.

You and Watson both get to your feet and stagger back to the office.

▶ *In the office – Turn to 67*

The word puzzle has reminded you of a previous adventure. "That business with Sir Henry involved a note like the one we received tonight, made out of newsprint letters," you say.

"You mean Lord Baskerville?" asks Watson, looking up from the unconscious man.

"Indeed, Watson. Although, this time I think there's more to this torn note than there was in that case. I believe it's been very carefully put together and, perhaps more to the point, tampered with after it was created."

This encourages you to look once more at the note (1) and consider all the letters that have a nick on the left-hand side.

On its own, the answer doesn't seem to make any sense. Perhaps if you discover more clues, a solution might begin to reveal itself.

Pushing the newspaper aside, you open the folder you took from the drawer marked "H". It contains a single piece of paper with a short message written on it.

▶ *Read the message – Turn to 52*

A TWISTED KNIFE

You call out to Watson over the noise of the engine – you have to shout – and he runs into the engine house to join you.

"The poor man," he says, crouching down beside the body of the engineer. Watson leans the dead man forward and looks at his back. He winces because even though he is a military man, he is still sensitive to brutality.

"One deep thrust from behind, and then the knife was twisted." He gently rests the body back against the wall, and stands up.

Steam hisses through the pipes around you. The engine is not running as smoothly as it should since the engineer stopped tending it. It's hard to tell how long he's been dead; maybe half an hour?

The hissing from the nearby pipes starts to alarm you. Pressure is building up and some of the steam is venting.

▶ *Inspect the pipes – Turn to 17*

3:30

You fold up the green plan, but as you do so you notice a handwritten note written on the back of it:

Superintendent
appointment.
Wednesday,
3:30pm

▶ *Smoke your pipe – Turn to 38*

COAL TUNNEL

These days, coal for the beam engines is delivered by railway, on the other side of the works. So, this tunnel running to barges on the river is not in regular use.

There are two iron rails here, once used to transport hand carts, hauled by rope and pushed from behind. But the tunnel is neglected. There is debris and forgotten props and planks piled near the entrance. Water drips from the patches of moss that have managed to grow in some of the mortar cracks. It forms puddles among the rails and sleepers, rippling around piles of spilled or discarded coal.

Mercifully, cables stretch along the tunnel walls and the lighting system is still operational. Sadly, the power only extends a little way into the tunnel. Beyond that, the light fades and the remainder of the passage is in darkness. For now, you make haste while you can see what's ahead of you.

The lamps on the ceiling cast their reflections in the pools of water, and your keen eye detects the mirrored images of Dancing Men ciphers that have been scratched into the rough rock in the ceiling of the coal tunnel.

This is a fiendish cipher indeed, more suited to a carnival hall of mirrors. But it is not beyond the wit of Sherlock Holmes to break the code.

► *Turn to the number hidden in the tunnel*

THE YARD

from 29

"Be alert Watson," you say, "these footprints suggest there is at least one more hoodlum at large than we can account for so far."

Your prudence is rewarded: when another hoodlum appears from beside a stack of barrels here in the yard – this one just as big and menacing as the giant stoker – you are not caught unawares. Mind you, you don't have a plan for dealing with him either, other than to run into the coal tunnel that you hope might have been overlooked. You can get there at a stretch, but then so can the big man.

You turn to the ever-resourceful Doctor Watson, who is pointing his service revolver directly at the hoodlum, now standing stock-still and slowly raising his hands in the air. You feel obliged to comment on the sudden appearance of the firearm.

"I didn't think you had brought your revolver, Watson," you say.

"Well," he replies, "I did."

At that moment the boiler house door flies off its hinges and the giant stoker steps through. You don't like the look of the manic grin playing on his lips.

But Watson has bought you enough time to cross the short distance to the concealed entrance of the tunnel, backing away from the hoodlums who follow a cautious distance away as Watson levels his gun at them. As the thugs come together you wonder, briefly, if they might be twins.

When you're close to the mouth of the tunnel, Watson lets loose a bullet. He aims at the ground between the two hoodlums to make them jump – which they do, albeit briefly – and you both turn and sprint into the black arch that offers, perhaps, a route to the river and escape.

▶ *Escape through coal tunnel – Turn to 102*

221B BAKER STREET

You sit down at your writing desk, light your pipe and inspect the note. Watson makes himself comfortable in a chair by the fire and waits for you to think things through. You examine the paper and the pasted letters, noting every detail and implication, and lean back as you think of what you know, and what you don't.

The message is clearly from that arch-villain Moriarty, who will inevitably be behind this. Sebastian Moran is his man, after all, and you know – because it is your business to know such things – that he is indeed currently incarcerated in Newgate. But where Moriarty is concerned, there is usually more to the matter.

You carefully slide the note back into its envelope and slip it into your pocket. (Feel free to refer to it at any time.)

You also make sure Watson has picked up his pocket notebook. It will be helpful if you need to record any clues from the events that are likely to unfold in the course of the night ahead of you. He also picks up his Periodic Table from the desk (this can be referred to at the back of the book).

You stand and clear your throat loudly. "Watson, shall we?"

You have spent so long sitting at your desk that the doctor's head has nodded forward and he is nearly asleep. He splutters slightly as he recovers.

"Shall I bring my revolver?" he asks, rising from the chair.

"Heavens no," you reply, "we're going a-spying, not killing." You grasp your coat from the coat-stand and stride out of the room, down the stairs, and out onto Baker Street. Half a minute later, Watson joins you.

You flag down a hansom cab. "Where to, sirs?" asks the driver.

▶ *"To Kew Bridge"* – Turn to 18

THE GREEN PLAN

You unfold the green plan and smooth it out. It appears to show possible sizes for square pipes on a site.

There are 16 equally spaced points marked on the plan in a 3 × 3 grid, and a table listing each of the possible sizes of square that can fit on it. The table hasn't been completed yet: only two square sizes have been shown.

One square has been drawn in blue ink and is 1 × 1. Another is 2 × 2, and has been drawn in red. Both those sizes have been added to the table. They could have been placed on the points in many different positions, but in each case just one example is enough to show that it is possible.

If every corner of a square must be on one of the 16 points, how many different sizes of square are possible?

Watson peers over your shoulder. "Well, I can see a third size straight away... it's very easy, isn't it?"

The square Watson sees is indeed easy: you saw it straight away too (it goes all around the outside, occupying an area of 9 units). But... is there another one? Or more?

In total, how many different sizes of square – with every corner on a marked point – can fit on the plan?

▶ *Exactly 3 – Turn to 44*

▶ *Exactly 4 – Turn to 101*

▶ *Exactly 5 – Turn to 95*

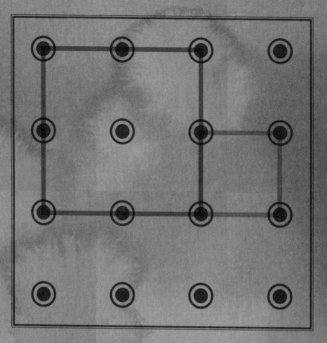

SQUARES ONLY, corners must be
on position marked ◉

Size	Possible?
1 X 1	yes
2 X 2	yes

PIPE PLAN

Grand Junction
Water Works.

A CURIOUS MARK

As you flick through the notebook you had previously thought empty, you spot a flash of red ink. You turn back a few pages and find it: a curious mark.

Discombobulate

► *Turn to the last page of the red notebook – Turn to 64*

(107) ELEMENTARY

"Good heavens, it IS blood," Watson announces, confidently.

"Are you sure about that Watson?" you respond, discouragingly.

► *Check again – Turn to 36*

(108) NO TIME TO LOSE

"Stop dithering, Holmes. It is most unlike you," snaps Watson.

► *Stop dithering – Turn to 60*

RASTROY'S LAUNDRY

from 18

It was very faint, but I could hear a feeble answering tattoo.

"Dit dit dit, dah dah dah, dit dit dit."

With a crow of triumph, Holmes shoved a laundry basket out of the way to reveal a trapdoor below.

"Help me, man!" he cried and together we heaved at the ring on the trap, forcing it open. We peered down into a long, low basement, full of un-laundry-like presses; and peering anxiously back up at us was a stooped, stick-like figure, wearing a green eyeshade, shackled to one of the presses.

"Mr Caslon Gill, I presume," said Sherlock suavely. He can't resist a theatrical flourish. "My name is Sherlock Holmes, and I have come to restore you to freedom."

"Thank God you are come, Mr Holmes! I despaired that my message would get through to anyone who would understand it. They have me trapped down here, they demand that I print counterfeit notes!"

We leapt down into the cellar, and Holmes began to unpick the padlock that fettered Mr Gill to the heavy printing press.

"Who brought you here, Mr Gill?" I asked. "Surely not Mrs Rastroy?"

"I've never seen her. I was kidnapped by some thugs outside the Mint, neither of them female."

Sherlock looked smug. " I'll wager Mrs Jemima Rastroy is no more. Watson, do take Mr Gill back to Baker Street. I'll telegraph Lestrade about this money-laundering enterprise – if he has his wits about him, he can pick them all up tonight. If I surmise correctly, there will be a distribution run this very evening. Monday is washday after all."

▶ *Turn to 46*

(110) A DEADLY DOOR

from 4

"I don't like the look of this, Holmes," says Watson grimly. "We can't hope to exit through here."

You examine the contraption again, being careful not to touch anything. It's clear that you can't get past the door without either disarming the trap or detonating the flasks – which you presume contain appropriate amounts of glycerol, sulphuric acid and nitric acid. Judging from the quantities there's enough here to blow away a whole man, and possibly two-thirds of his loyal doctor companion too if he is stood as close as he is standing now.

You deduce that the clock-face at the centre of the device is the key. If you set the hands to the right time, you'll be able to open the door without it blowing up. You just need to pick the right time, and you haven't yet calculated what that is... so you won't be getting out any time soon.

Don't forget to ask Watson to keep a note of any times in his notebook.

▶ *Walk back to the office to look for more clues – Turn to 78*

▶ *Attempt to disarm the contraption manually – Turn to 6*

(111) TRAPPED

from 5

You awaken to find yourself in what appears to be an office. A clock on the desk indicates you've been out for hours. Watson, still unconscious, is lying on the floor next to you. There are four doors leading off from this room, but unsurprisingly, you find them all locked. Someone doesn't want you to leave. You could look for clues, but the cosh to the head has left you feeling dazed and not quite yourself.

▶ *Wait for Watson to wake up – Turn to 67*

A CARTFUL OF COAL

from 60

The door is in shadow, but your eyes are keen enough to spot some dark splashes on the stone steps leading up to them. Beyond the door, you can hear the muffled rhythm of the working engines. Watson tries the handle with his gloved hand; it turns easily. As soon as he pushes the door open, the sound of the steam engines surges through. You both step quickly inside and Watson shuts the door behind you, as fast as he can without slamming it. You've taken only two steps away from the door when there is a commotion outside as someone – the watchman, perhaps? – rams a heavy object against the other side of it. A tumbling percussion follows, sounding suspiciously like a cartful of coal being suddenly unloaded. The clamour abruptly dies down, and Watson tries the door. The handle turns but – exactly as you knew it would not – the door won't shift. The good doctor throws his shoulder against it, but it moves not an inch.

Watson walks forward into the centre of the entrance hall. But you're looking at the ground, where there are more splashes of dark liquid on the flagstone by your feet. You stoop down, touch it with your finger, and sniff.

You look for more splashes. They are just where you anticipated them to be: dotting a path to the open office door straight ahead of you.

Watson looks back at you. "Good heavens, Holmes! Is it blood?"

"If I'm correct, the chemical makeup of this is lead, cadmium, chromium, manganese, cobalt, arsenic, bismuth, and molybdenum."

"Oh goodness! Something more serious then?" says Watson. He looks worried as he flicks through his notebook to his Periodic Table.

▶ *The sum of the atomic numbers are even – Turn to 36*

▶ *The sum of the atomic numbers are odd – Turn to 107*

HiNts

aNd

SOLutIoNS

221A – HINTS

(1) 221B Baker Street

There are three numbers hidden in the torn note – you'll find clues to these in three different places (and the solutions are linked, by entry-number when you find each one, later in this section).

Someone appears to have tampered with the note before delivering it, so there is also a secret message. You'll need to find three explicit key clues before you can extract that message from the note, and you'll only find those clues if you get other puzzles right.

(3) Moriarty's Hoodlums

There are a number of ways to approach this problem. Here's one: pick one of the four methods of killing, and try to work out how many hoodlums can possibly know it. That's easier than it sounds because you know it must be a single hoodlum skilled in each of the other methods... and you know exactly how many other methods there are. It's going to be the same for each of the methods, so once you've worked out how many hoodlums know each method, you're almost there...

(7) A Half-Finished Word Puzzle

As you start to solve the word puzzle, you should notice that they are in fact all titles of Sherlock Holmes adventures. If you find all those, you'll have half of the letters of 9 across. That should be enough to deduce a word, which is itself from the title of one of Holmes' most famous cases.

(14) The Black Notebook

Maybe a "mixed-up clue" is an anagram? Although there's nothing on the cover or the notepad, there is something relevant on the cover of another book you know all about.

(16) The Sumatran Rat Puzzle

Check each rat carefully. It's easier than it looks. Does this puzzle hold the key?

(17) **The Pressure Gauge Puzzle**
A broken gauge's dial has no number shown on it. But if you know the totals of the dials connected to the outputs below it (left and right), you can add them together to get the value of that gauge's dial. So a good place to start is to find a gauge that has numbers shown on both of the two dials below it.

Remember that sometimes more than one pipe combine, so you need to add two numbers together for an output dial, rather than splitting the number into two.

(18) **The Tower**
Not all those winged animals are birds. Identify which are bats and which are crows.

(22) **A Maze in a Drawer**
Try to find the route through it!

(23) **A Secret Message**
This is a special clue. Maybe you should record it in Watson's Notebook?

(24) **A Race Against Time**
Try all the routes! It's a process of elimination.

(25) **The Underlined Letters**
Inspect every letter in turn, reading the note naturally (from top left to bottom right), and find only those which are underlined.

(27) **A Code in the Floorboards**
This is "just" a decoding puzzle using the Code Wheel. If your Code Wheel is broken, there's an online version you can use at: www.ammonitepress. com/gift/sherlock-code-wheel

(29) Footprints

You've already seen two of the prints in detail – the engineer's murderer and the stoker. So, if you can identify the characteristics of their boots, you can isolate any prints that don't belong to those two. Can all those prints be attributed to a single pair of boots?

(32) A Narrow Escape

Inspect every letter in turn, reading the note naturally (from top left to bottom right), and find only those which have a small tear on the bottom edge.

(36) The Main Office

This is practice for using the Code Wheel on the cover of the book. Make sure the letter H appears in the Input Letter, and read the number that is revealed. If your Code Wheel is broken, there's an online version you can use at: www.ammonitepress.com/gift/sherlock-code-wheel

(40) An Elementary Code

Add the chemical symbols to the labels, and see what emerges.

(43) Inventory

There's more than one way to solve this, but one method requires you to dust off your algebra. The key thing is that, after distribution, all the bins have the same weight. Furthermore, because one item from each bin was put into each of the other bins, you know that each bin has 3 fewer items (because whichever bin you pick, there are 3 "other bins") than the inventory stated, plus one of each of the other items. So, using h as an individual hook, B for a wide bolt, b for a long bolt, and w for a washer, you can say this:

$$(2 \times h) + B + b + w = h + (5 \times B) + b + w = h + B + (7 \times b) + w = h + B + b + (97 \times w)$$

(46) The Daily Gazette

The punched-out letters are from the following words: COURT, GRIEF, PAVEMENT, EXTREME, JOURNEY, CORRESPONDENCE, JANUARY.

The letters need to be decoded using the Code Wheel to spell out an anagram of a one-word number.

(54) The Maudslay Engine Room

Why don't you look above the engine?

(56) The Magic Square

If only two numbers have been swapped, you can still work out what the rows or columns should add up to. The rows and columns that don't have the misplaced numbers in them will add up to the same number, so if you add enough up you should be able to find it. Once you've found that number, you can start to isolate the rows and columns that don't work, either by using trial-and-error or actually calculating the differences in sums.

(58) A Red Notebook

If you don't trust your maths to calculate the answer, try writing out 32 numbers skipping every fourth number. What number do you end up on?

(64) Names in a Grid

No hint! Is Moriarty present or not?

(70) A Burst of Inspiration

Find the letters in the torn note with a nick at the top. This is a special clue. Maybe you should record it in your notebook?

(72) The Boiler House

Look for the Dancing Men. When you've found them all, rearrange the letters they represent into a number.

(74) The Clockmaker's Conundrum

The one time you know the clock hands line up is at six o'clock. Because clock hands travel at a constant rate (that's a predictable and essential feature of a clock!) this happens at a constant interval, so they must line up in this way regularly. If you can work out the number of times in the 12-hour cycle this happens, you can calculate the times because they must be evenly distributed.

(76) A Precise Time

Inspect every letter on pink paper in turn, reading the note naturally (from top left to bottom right), and find only those which were torn out of a document in pink paper.

(79) A Blueprint

First you need to put the map together (maybe draw that on another piece of paper). Check the three mappings: 1, 4 and 5. If any one of them does not lead to the stated encoded letter, you don't have to check any more: you only need to know if all of them are correct, so as soon as you find one that isn't, you can stop.

(80) A Number of Hoodlums

There are a number of ways to approach this problem. Here's one: pick one of the four methods of killing, and try to work out how many hoodlums can possibly know it. That's easier than it sounds because you know it must be a single hoodlum skilled in each of the other methods... and you know exactly how many other methods there are. It's going to be the same for each of the methods, so once you've worked out how many hoodlums know each method, you're almost there...

(86) Setting the Hands

Consider all the times you've encountered so far. Can you see the pattern linking them? Be aware that it's possible that the times you recorded may be wrong if they were the result of a wrong answer in another puzzle.

(90) **Boulton & Watt Engine Room**

Look for six Dancing Men. When you have them, decrypt them using the Code Wheel. Solve the anagram: it leads to a number (of course).

(96) **The Code of the Foreman's Hand**

Follow the instructions carefully, being sure to start at X. To unlock the safe, you need to turn the number of places shown by the number on the Code Wheel, changing direction (anticlockwise/clockwise) each time.

Finally, remember to read the Output Letter off the Code Wheel, and then set the Input Letter of the Code Wheel to reveal a colour.

(99) **Lord Baskerville**

Look for letters with a nick to the left. This is a special clue. Maybe you should record it in your notebook?

(102) **Coal Tunnel**

Remember that the Dancing Men you're seeing are an upside-down and mirror-imaged reflection of the actual marks you need to decode. Be careful because sometimes figures in the Dancing Men code really are standing on their heads. Once you've got the Dancing Men, you'll need to decode them using the Code Wheel.

(105) **The Green Plan**

Remember this puzzle is about finding how many different-sized squares can fit, not how many squares there are (for example, there are nine of the 1×1 squares, but that's only one size). Although the corners of the square must be on the circles (which also means that the squares cannot hang outside the boundary shown), the edges don't necessarily have to align with the vertical/horizontal grid...

(112) **A Cartful of Coal**

Find the elements in the Periodic Table and add together their atomic numbers.

221B – SOLUTIONS

(1) 221B Baker Street
The secrets in the torn note are the only ones whose solution is not revealed.

(3) Moriarty's Hoodlums
Each method of killing is known by a hoodlum skilled in each of the other methods, of which there are three – so must be known by 3 hoodlums. Since there are four methods in total, that makes $3 \times 4 = 12$ hoodlums. But you know that every hoodlum knows two (and only two) methods, which means that you've counted each hoodlum twice. So halve the total and you get the answer: Moriarty has 6 hoodlums. Therefore, the solution is "Fewer than 7".

(7) A Half-Finished Word Puzzle
The 7th letter of 9 across is V (which maps to YELLOW in the Code Wheel).

The missing solutions are:
Across: 1 Red Circle, 9 Baskervilles, 14 Blanched Soldier
Down: 1 Cardboard Box, 2 Crooked Man, 4 Devil's Foot,
6 Sussex Vampire, 8 Three Gables, 12 Speckled Band.

Anachronism: Although Holmes may have been familiar with other word puzzles, crossword puzzles like this did not really appear in newspapers until around 1920.

(14) The Black Notebook
Only one of the three phrases is an anagram of "Ormond Sacker", whose name appears on the cover of this book.

(16) The Sumatran Rat Puzzle
Yes, every rat has a twin.

If you also found and understood the secret message in the torn note, you should have realized that this rat puzzle is the Sumatran Rat Problem to which it referred.

(17) **The Pressure Gauge Puzzle**

The final dial is 24. The two dials feeding into it must be 18 and 6.

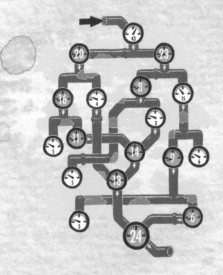

(18) **The Tower**

There are an 14 crows and 5 bats.

(22) **A Maze in a Drawer**

This maze has no route through it, so you can't solve it in 15 seconds. That's okay though, provided you choose the answer that says you can't.

(23) **A Secret Message**

This is one of three clues that you can use to thwart Moriarty. Someone has bravely tampered with the torn note and hidden a message in there to help you succeed. When you have all three such clues (each marked with a key symbol), revisit the torn note you were given at the start.

24 A Race Against Time

25 The Underlined Letters

The letters spell out FORTY EIGHT (48).

27 A Code in the Floorboards

The Dancing Men spell out FIFTY ONE (51).

29 Footprints

There are four pairs of boots that made the prints.

32 A Narrow Escape

The letters with a nick below spell out TWENTY SEVEN (27).

36 The Main Office

H maps to 7.

(40) An Elementary Code

The symbols for the elements are:
Thorium (Th); Rheniun (Re); Einsteinium (Es); Carbon (C); Oxygen (O);
Tungsten (W); Iodine (I); Nickel (Ni); Neon (Ne); Molybdenum (Mo).

Arranged in the order described, with duplicates, gives:
Th Re Es C O Re W I Th Ni Ne Mo Re
THREE SCORE WITH NINE MORE = (3 x 20) + 9 = 69

Anachronism: As hinted at the puzzle, some of these chemicals (by
these names... and hence their symbols) are anachronistic in the 1800s.
Furthermore, Einsteinium (for example) can't be found casually in bottles
like this even today, as it's synthetically produced in tiny quantities, decays
rapidly and is dangerously radioactive.

(43) Inventory

The relative values are:
1 hook = 4 wide bolts = 6 long bolts = 96 washers.
You don't know their exact weights, but you can be sure of these relative
values. So the answer is that 1 hook is "as heavy as 6 long bolts".

This puzzle is actually very old: it appeared, using gems instead of industrial
pieces, in *The Lilavati*, an Indian book on arithmetic written in the 12th
century.

(46) The Daily Gazette

The letters spell out FIFTEEN (15).

(54) The Maudslay Engine Room

The number hidden in the illustration, to the right of the pale pipe in the
top-right corner, is 71.

(56) **The Magic Square**

Numbers 12 and 16 have been swapped over, so the answer (12 + 16) is 28.

12	3	2	13
5	10	11	8
9	6	7	16
4	15	14	1

(58) **A Red Notebook**

The page number on the last page is 42. Here's the whole sequence, with pages where the number was skipped marked in bold:

1, 2, 3, 4, 5, 6, 7, **8**, 9, 10, 11, **12**, 13, 14, 15, **16**, 17, 18, 19, **20**, 21, 22, 23, **24**, 25, 26, 27, **28**, 29, 30, 31, **32**, 33, 34, 35, **36**, 37, 38, 39, **40** , 41, 42.

(64) **Names in a Grid**

"MORIARTY" does not appear in the word puzzle.

Anachronism: wordsearch puzzles like this are really much too modern for Holmes to have ever seen one in this form.

(70) **A Burst of Inspiration**

Letters with a nick above them is one of three clues that you can use to thwart Moriarty. Someone has bravely tampered with the torn note and hidden a message in there to help you succeed. When you have all three such clues, revisit the torn note you were given at the start.

(72) The Boiler House

The Dancing Men spell out 4.

F O U R

(74) The Clockmaker's Conundrum

The precise times that hands line up pointing in different directions (ignoring seconds) are:

12:32, 1:38, 2:43, 3:49, 4:54, 6:00, 7:05, 8:10, 9:16, 10:21, 11:27

Answer: after 10:21, the first time two hands line up in this way is at 11:27 (and 16 seconds). So, two hours before that is 9:27.

(76) A Precise Time

The letters spell out THIRTY NINE (39).

(79) A Blueprint

All the pipes (Number = Input Letter = Output Letter): 1 = D = Y, 2 = A = P, 3 = E = V, 4 = B = W, 5 = C = T. So, the mappings are correct.

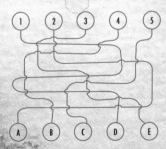

(80) A Number of Hoodlums

Each method of killing is known by a hoodlum skilled in each of the other methods, of which there are three - so must be known by 3 hoodlums. Since there are four methods in total, that makes $3 \times 4 = 12$ hoodlums. But you know that every hoodlum knows two (and only two) methods - which means that you've counted each hoodlum twice. So halve the total and you get the answer: Moriarty has 6 hoodlums. Therefore, the solution is "Fewer than 7".

(86) Setting the Hands

If you've proceeded through the other puzzles correctly, you'll have seen four times (the time the governor was abducted, the time on the carriage clock in the office, the result of the clock-hands-pointing-away-from-each-other puzzle, and the train ticket you found in the boiler house).

Furthermore, Watson will have pointed out that the carriage clock is running slow, so you need to modify that time accordingly. Unfortunately, if you got some puzzles wrong along the way, you may have been shown some unhelpful times too, which make it hard or impossible for you to solve this.

If you look at the times you have, you can notice that they are all 2 hours and 24 minutes apart – apart from one gap which is 4 hours 48 minutes (twice that). That is, you should have four times and you can calculate the fifth one like this:

2:15 + 2 hours and 24 minutes – time on discarded train ticket
4:39 + 2 hours and 24 minutes – SOLUTION
7:03 + 2 hours and 24 minutes – time governor was abducted
9:27 + 2 hours and 24 minutes – result of the clock puzzle
11:51 + 2 hours and 24 minutes – time on clock in office (after correcting for it running 10 minutes slow)

4:39 is the time you need to set on the booby trap.

90 Boulton & Watt Engine Room

The Dancing Men can be decoded using the Code Wheel to spell out 12.

C B J Q E J
T W E L V E

96 The Code of the Foreman's Hand

The pattern is:
Start at X. Anticlockwise 6 letters, stops at D.
Clockwise 1 letter, stops at C.
Anticlockwise 7 letters, stops at J.
Clockwise 3 letters, stops at G.
The Code Wheel encrypts G to I...
So finally set the wheel to I, which shows BLUE.

99 Lord Baskerville

Letters with a nick on the left offer one of three clues that you can use to thwart Moriarty. Someone has bravely tampered with the torn note and hidden a message in there to help you succeed. When you have all three such clues, revisit the torn note you were given at the start.

102 Coal Tunnel

The Dancing Men can be decoded to spell out 61.

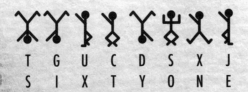

T G U C D S X J
S I X T Y O N E

(105) The Green Plan

There are 5 different sizes of square that satisfy the criteria. The diagram shows the area of these different sizes, with an example of each drawn on the plan.

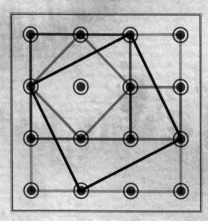

SQUARES ONLY, corners must be on position marked ⦿	
Size	Possible?
☐ 1 X 1	yes
☐ 2 X 2	yes
☐ 3 X 3	yes
☐ √2 X √2	yes
◼ √5 X √5	yes

(112) A Cartful of Coal

The atomic numbers are: lead (82), cadmium (48), chromium (24), manganese (25), cobalt (27), arsenic (33), bismuth (83), and molybdenum (42). These add up to 364, an even number.

Did you discover the hidden Sherlock Holmes passages?
If not, they can be found on the following pages:

15 – taken from *The Adventure of the Gloria Scott* (1893)
51 – taken from *The Adventure of the Dancing Men* (1903)

PERIODIC TABLE

| 1 H Hydrogen | | | | | | | | | |

| 3 Li Lithium | 4 Be Beryllium |
| 11 Na Sodium | 12 Mg Magnesium |

19 K Potassium	20 Ca Calcium	21 Sc Scandium	22 Ti Titanium	23 V Vanadium	24 Cr Chromium	25 Mn Manganese	26 Fe Iron	27 Co Cobalt
37 Rb Rubidium	38 Sr Strontium	39 Y Yttrium	40 Zr Zirconium	41 Nb Niobium	42 Mo Molybdenum	43 Tc Technetium	44 Ru Ruthenium	45 Rh Rhodium
55 Cs Cesium	56 Ba Barium		72 Hf Hafnium	73 Ta Tantalum	74 W Tungsten	75 Re Rhenium	76 Os Osmium	77 Ir Iridium
87 Fr Francium	88 Ra Radium		104 Rf Rutherfordium	105 Db Dubnium	106 Sg Seaborgium	107 Bh Bohrium	108 Hs Hassium	109 Mt Meitnerium

| 57 La Lanthanum | 58 Ce Cerium | 59 Pr Praseodymium | 60 Nd Neodymium | 61 Pm Promethium | 62 Sm Samarium |
| 89 Ac Actinium | 90 Th Thorium | 91 Pa Protactinium | 92 U Uranium | 93 Np Neptunium | 94 Pu Plutonium |

NOTES

....

....

....

							2 He Helium
5 B Boron	6 C Carbon	7 N Nitrogen	8 O Oxygen	9 F Fluorine	10 Ne Neon

5 B Boron	6 C Carbon	7 N Nitrogen	8 O Oxygen	9 F Fluorine	10 Ne Neon
13 Al Aluminium	14 Si Silicon	15 P Phosphorus	16 S Sulfur	17 Cl Chlorine	18 Ar Argon

28 Ni Nickel	29 Cu Copper	30 Zn Zinc	31 Ga Gallium	32 Ge Germanium	33 As Arsenic	34 Se Selenium	35 Br Bromine	36 Kr Krypton
46 Pd Palladium	47 Ag Silver	48 Cd Cadmium	49 In Indium	50 Sn Tin	51 Sb Antimony	52 Te Tellurium	53 I Iodine	54 Xe Xenon
78 Pt Platinum	79 Au Gold	80 Hg Mercury	81 Tl Thallium	82 Pb Lead	83 Bi Bismuth	84 Po Polonium	85 At Astatine	86 Rn Radon
110 Ds Darmstadtium	111 Rg Roentgenium	112 Cn Copernicum	113 Uut Ununtrium	114 Fl Flerovium	115 Uup Ununperntium	116 Lv Livermorium	117 Uus Ununseptium	118 Uuo Ununoctium

63 Eu Europium	64 Gd Gadolinium	65 Tb Terbium	66 Dy Dysprosium	67 Ho Holmium	68 Er Erbium	69 Tm Thulium	70 Yb Ytterbium	71 Lu Lutetium
95 Am Americium	96 Cm Curium	97 Bk Berkelium	98 Cf Californium	99 Es Einsteinium	100 Fm Fermium	101 Md Mendelevium	102 No Nobelium	103 Lr Lawrencium

First published 2019 by
Ammonite Press
an imprint of Guild of Master Craftsman Publications Ltd
Castle Place, 166 High Street, Lewes, East Sussex, BN7 1XU,
United Kingdom

Reprinted 2019, 2020,2021, 2022, 2023

ISBN 978-1-78145-348-3

Publisher: Jonathan Bailey
Designer: Robin Shields
Editor: Jamie Pumfrey
Additional Text: Viv Croot

Colour reproduction by GMC Reprographics
Printed and bound in China

With special thanks to the London Museum of Water and Steam
www.waterandsteam.org.uk

If you've escaped the pages (or are still trapped!)
send us a message: **#SherlockHolmesEscapeBook**
@ammonitepress

AMMONITE
PRESS

www.ammonitepress.com